Chasing the Wind

Chasing the Wind

By
William MacDonald

MOODY PRESS
CHICAGO

ISBN: 0-8024-1246-7

All Scriptures quoted in this book are from the *New American Standard Version,* except where indicated otherwise.

The use of selected references from various versions of the Bible in this publication does not necessarily imply publisher endorsement of the versions in their entirety.

Second Printing, 1976

Printed in the United States of America

CONTENTS

ABBREVIATIONS

My comments are based upon the text of various versions of the Bible, principally the New American Standard Bible. The following is the key to the abbreviations used:

ASV	American Standard Version (1901)
JND	New Translation by J. N. Darby
KJV	King James Version
NASB	New American Standard Bible
NEB	New English Bible
TEV	The New Testament in Today's English Version
TLB	The Living Bible

INTRODUCTION

Search for Reality

At one time in his life, Solomon set out to find the true meaning of human existence. He was determined to discover the good life. Richly endowed with wisdom and comfortably cushioned by wealth (1 Ki 10:14-25; 2 Ch 9:22-24), he thought that if anyone could find lasting satisfaction, he was the one. Like many of our contemporaries, he sought the answer to the haunting question, "Is there life after birth?"

But there was a self-imposed condition to Solomon's search. He was going to do this on his own. He hoped that his own I.Q. would enable him to discover fulfillment in life, quite apart from divine revelation. It would be the exploration of a man without any help from the supreme Deity. He would search "under the sun" for the greatest good in life.

UNDER THE SUN

The phrase, *under the sun,* forms the most important single key to understanding the book of Ecclesiastes. The fact that it occurs twenty-nine times indicates the general perspective of the author. His search is confined to this earth. He ransacks the world to solve the riddle of life. And his whole quest is carried on by his own mind, unaided by God.

If this key—*under the sun*—is not kept constantly in mind, then the book will present mountainous difficulties. It will seem to contradict the rest of Scripture, to set forth strange doctrines, and to advocate a morality that is questionable, to say the least.

But if we remember that the book is a compendium of human, not divine, wisdom, then we will understand why it is that while some of Solomon's conclusions are true, some are only half true, and some are not true at all. Let us take some illustrations. Ecclesiastes 12:1 is true and dependable advice for young people in all ages; they should remember their Creator in the days of their youth. Verse 4 of chapter 1 is only half true; it is true that one generation follows another, but it is not true that the earth remains forever (see Ps 102:25-26 and 2 Pe 3:7, 10). And the following statements, if taken at face value, are not true at all: "There is nothing better for a man than to eat and drink and tell himself that his labor is good" (2:24); "There is no advantage for man over beast" (3:19); and "The dead do not know anything" (9:5). But if we did not have any revelation from God, we would probably arrive at the same conclusions.

Is the Book Inspired?

When we say that some of Solomon's conclusions "under the sun" are only half true and that some are not true at all, what does this do to the inspiration of Ecclesiastes? The answer, of course, is that it does not affect the question of inspiration in the slightest.

The book is part of the inspired Word of God. It is God-breathed in the sense that the Lord ordained that it should be included in the canon of Scripture. We hold to the verbal, plenary inspiration of Ecclesiastes as we do to the rest of the Bible.

But the inspired books of the Bible often contain statements by Satan or by men which are not true. In Genesis 3:4, for instance, the devil told Eve that she would not die if she ate the fruit of the tree in the middle of the garden. It was a lie, but it is quoted in the Scripture to teach us that the devil has been a liar from the beginning. "Inspiration may record the untruth of Satan (or of men) but it does not vindicate the lie or sanctify it. It secures the exact record of what was said—good or bad."[1]

So we should not be surprised to find half-truths or untruths in a book which is clearly labelled as containing man's wisdom "under the sun." It should not affect our confidence in the trustworthiness of the Bible.

What Did Solomon Decide?

Solomon's search for meaning ended with the dismal conclusion that life is vanity and vexation of spirit (1:14), or, better, a striving after wind. As far as he was able to determine, life under the sun simply wasn't worth the effort. He wasn't able to find fulfillment or lasting satisfaction. In spite of all his wealth and wisdom, he failed to discover the good life.

And of course his conclusion was right. If one never gets *above* the sun, life is an exercise in futility. It is meaningless. Everything that the world has to offer, put together, cannot satisfy the heart of man. It was Pascal who said, "There is a God-shaped vacuum in the human heart." And Augustine observed, "Thou hast made us, O Lord, for Thyself, and our heart shall find no rest till it rest in Thee."

Solomon's experience anticipated the truth of the words of the Lord Jesus, "Everyone who drinks of this water shall thirst again" (Jn 4:13). The water of this world cannot provide lasting satisfaction.

We believe that Solomon's search for reality was only a temporary phase, a single chapter in his biography. We do not know how old he was when he embarked on this philosophical quest for truth, but apparently he was an older man when he wrote this diary of it (1:12; 11:9). Eventually Solomon did get his sights above the sun and became a true believer; this seems evident from the fact that the greater part of three books of the Bible are attributed to him. However, the sin and failure which clouded the closing years of his life remind us how seriously a believer can backslide, and how imperfect even the most brilliant types of the Lord Jesus are.

BUT DIDN'T HE BELIEVE IN GOD?

It is obvious that Solomon believed in the existence of God, even during the time when he was searching for fulfillment. He makes no less than forty references to God in the book of Ecclesiastes. But this does not mean that he was a devout believer at that time. The name of God which he uses throughout is Elohim, the name which reveals Him as the Mighty Creator. Not once does he refer to God as Jehovah, the God who enters into covenant relationship with man.

This is an important observation. Man under the sun can know that there is a God. As Paul reminds us in Romans 1:20: "For since the creation of the world His invisible attributes, His eternal power and divine nature, have been clearly seen, being understood through what has been made, so that they are without excuse. The existence of God is obvious from creation. Atheism is not a mark of wisdom but of willful blindness. Solomon, the wisest man who ever lived, groping for truth with his own mind, acknowledged the fact of a Supreme Being.

But while Elohim can be known by man under the sun, Jehovah can only be known through special revelation. So the repeated references to God in this book should not be equated with saving faith. All they prove is that creation witnesses to the existence of God, and that men who deny it are fools (Ps 14:1; 53:1).

DID SOLOMON REALLY WRITE THE BOOK?

It will come as a surprise to some to learn that many Bible scholars doubt that Solomon was the author of Ecclesiastes. That is surprising because the internal evidence of his authorship seems so clear. The writer identifies himself as the son of David and king over Israel in Jerusalem (1:1, 12). This clearly seems to point to Solomon. Other internal references identify him as wise and wealthy, as sponsoring vast building projects, and as having almost limitless opportunities for pleasure. All these descriptions fit Solomon perfectly.

But the scholars come back with the argument that many words and grammatical constructions found in the book were not in use when Solomon lived but belong to the period after the Babylonian captivity. And in reply to the internal evidences cited above, they contend that it was a legitimate literary device for some later writer to put his words in Solomon's mouth.

The arguments pro and con are lengthy and involved, and we cannot go into them here. It is sufficient to say that none of the objections that have been raised against Solomonic authorship are insuperable. Responsible scholars, such as Gleason Archer, show that to believe that Solomon wrote the book is still a live option.[2]

<h2 style="text-align:center">WHY WAS IT WRITTEN?</h2>

The question inevitably arises, "Why did God ordain that a book which never rises above the sun should be included in the Holy Bible?"

The answer is this: the book was included so that no one will ever have to live through Solomon's dismal experience, searching for satisfaction where it cannot be found.

Natural man instinctively thinks he can make himself happy through possessions, or pleasure, or travel on the one hand, or through drugs or liquor or sexual indulgence on the other. But the message of this book is that someone wiser and wealthier than most of us will ever be has tried and failed. So we can save ourselves all the expense and heartache and frustration and disappointment by looking above the sun to the One who alone can satisfy—the Lord Jesus Christ. Kris Kristofferson mirrored the purpose of Ecclesiastes when he wrote, "Maybe, Lord, I can show someone else what I've been through on my way to You."

THE CULTS LOVE IT

Ecclesiastes is one of the favorite books of the false cults. They quote it with great enthusiasm to prove their heretical doctrines, especially doctrines dealing with death and the hereafter. For instance, they use verses from this book to teach soul-sleep after death and the annihilation of the wicked dead. They wrench verses out of context to deny the immortality of the soul and the doctrine of eternal punishment.

But they never put the key in the door. They never tell their victims that Ecclesiastes expounds man's wisdom under the sun and therefore is not a valid source of proof texts for doctrines of the Christian faith.

JOIN THE CLUB

If you find Ecclesiastes to be unusually difficult to understand, join the club. At times, Solomon's conclusions appear contradictory. There does not seem to be any logical sequence to many of his observations. Some of his statements are so obscure that they have been the despair of commentators. His teaching is often so confusing that we too are tempted to throw up our hands in desperation.

But perhaps that is part of the grand design of the book. Remember that this is the record of a man who is groping for meaning. It is a book of human wisdom, not revelation. Man's philosophies do not characteristically make for easy reading. One who is searching for truth under the sun can scarcely be expected to write with the same clarity and definiteness as one who has found the truth.

So, as we now turn to a verse-by-verse study of the book, let us keep in mind its scope and perspective. This will save us from comparing it unfavorably with the other books of the Bible.

1

The Futility of It All

The author introduces himself in verse 1 of chapter 1 as the Preacher, the son of David, King in Jerusalem. That word *Preacher* is interesting. The Hebrew equivalent is *koheleth,* and it means "caller" or "congregator." The Greek is *ecclesiastes,* meaning, "one who convenes an assembly." From there it has been variously interpreted as meaning "convener, assembler, speaker, debater, spokesman, and preacher."

The Preacher was the son of David. While *son* here could admittedly mean a grandson or an even later descendant, the first sense probably makes the best sense. Solomon was the only descendant of David who was king over Israel in Jerusalem (v. 12). All the rest were kings over Judah. Those of other dynasties who were kings over Israel used Shechem (1 Ki 12:25) or Samaria (1 Ki 16:24) and not Jerusalem as their capital.

Solomon comes to the point right away (v. 2); we don't have to wait till we get to the last chapter. The result of all of Solomon's investigation and research under the sun is that all is vanity. Life is transitory, fleeting, useless, empty, and futile. It has no meaning. Nothing on this earth provides a valid goal of existence.

Is that true? Yes, it is absolutely true! If this life is all, if death draws a final curtain on human existence, then life is nothing but a vapor—unsubstantial and evanescent.

The apostle Paul reminds us that the whole creation was subjected to vanity or futility as a result of the entrance of sin (Ro 8:20). And it is not without significance that the first parents named their second son Abel, which means vanity. Solomon is right. All is vanity under the sun.

Solomon observed in verse 3 that frail man's life is filled with labor and activity, but where does it get him when all is said and done? He is on a treadmill, a tiresome round of motion without progress. You ask him why he works, and he replies, "To get money, of course." But why does he want money? To buy food. And why does he want food? To maintain his strength. Yes, but why does he want strength? He wants strength so he can work. And so there he is, right back where he began. He works to get money to buy food to get strength to work to get money to buy food to get strength, and so on, ad infinitum. As Henry Thoreau observed, he lives a life of quiet desperation.

Seeing a woman crying at a bus stop, a Christian asked her if he could be of any help. "Oh," she replied, "I'm just weary and bored. My husband is a hard worker, but he doesn't earn as much as I want. So I went to work. I get up early every morning, fix breakfast for our four children, pack lunches, and take a bus to my job. Then I return home for more drudgery, a few hours of sleep, and another day just like the one before. I guess I'm just sick of this endless routine."

It was H. L. Mencken who said, "The basic fact about human experience is not that it is a tragedy, but that it is a bore. It is not that it is predominately painful, but that it is lacking in any sense."[1]

The transience of men stands in stark contrast to the seeming permanence of his natural environment (v. 4). Generation succeeds generation with irresistible momentum. This is life under the sun.

Each one dreams that he will be enduring,
How soon that one becomes the missing face![2]
WILL H. HOUGHTON

"But the earth remains for ever." Apart from revelation, we might think that the present earth will last forever. That is what Solomon concludes. But Peter tells us that the earth and the works that are upon it will be burned up in the coming day of the Lord (2 Pe 3:10).

In verse 5, Solomon pointed out that nature moves in a continuous, inexorable cycle. For instance, the sun rises in the East, swings through the heavens to set in the West, then hurries around the other side of the world to rise in the East again. This seemingly endless pattern, age after age, makes man realize that he is nothing but a passing shadow.

If any are tempted to accuse Solomon of a scientific blunder for describing the sun as moving when actually it is the earth that moves in relation to the sun, they should hold their fire. He was merely using the language of human appearance. The sun *appears* to rise and set. We use this language all the time, and it is so readily understood that it should not require explanation.

Solomon continues the thought into verse 6. The wind patterns change with the same regularity as the seasons of the year. In the winter, the north winds sweep down over Israel to the Negev, the desert in the south. Then when summer comes, the south winds carry warmth on their northward flights. With almost dreary sameness, they follow these circuits, and then, with callous disregard for the world of men, pass off the scene.

Not only the earth, the sun, and the wind, but the water follows its same monotonous routine throughout the centuries (v. 7). The rivers flow down into the oceans but never to the point where the oceans overflow. For the sun evaporates enormous quantities of water. Then as the air cools, the vapor condenses and forms clouds. The clouds in turn scud across the skies and drop the water over the land areas in the form of rain, snow, or hail. And as the rivers are fed with the surplus, they bear the water back to the ocean. The ceaseless activity of nature reminds man of his own unending labor. Perhaps Kristofferson had Ecclesiastes 1:7 in mind when he wrote, "I'm just a river that rolled forever and never got to the sea."

Thus the life that is confined to this earth is full of weariness. Human language is inadequate to describe the monotony, boredom, and futility of it all (v.8). Man is never satisfied. No matter how much he sees, he still wants more. And his ears never reach the stage where they don't want to hear something new. He travels incessantly and frenetically for new sensations, new sights, new sounds. He is after what an American sociologist calls the fundamental wish for new experience. But he returns dissatisfied and jaded. Man is so constituted that all the world cannot bring lasting happiness to his heart. This does not mean that his case is hopeless. All he needs to do is get above the sun to the One who "satisfieth the longing soul, and filleth the hungry soul with goodness" (Ps 107:9, KJV).

> Worldly joy is fleeting—vanity itself;
> Vain the dazzling brightness, vain the stores of wealth;
> Vain the pomp and glory; only Thou canst give
> Peace and satisfaction while on earth we live.
> There is none, Lord Jesus, there is none like Thee
> For the soul that thirsteth, there is none like Thee.[3]
>
> AUTHOR UNKNOWN

An additional feature of Solomon's disillusionment was the discovery that there is nothing new under the sun (vv. 9-10). History is constantly repeating itself. He longed for new thrills, but before long, he found everything was, in its own way, a bad trip.

Is there really nothing new? Yes, in a sense, this is true. Even the most modern discoveries are developments of principles that were locked into creation at the beginning. Many of man's most boasted achievements have their counterparts in nature. Birds flew long before man did, for instance. Even space travel is not new. Enoch and Elijah were transported through space without even having to carry their own oxygen supplies with them! So those who spend their lives searching for novelties are bound to be disappointed. It has all happened before, long before we were born (v. 10).

Another bitter pill that man has to swallow, in verse 11, is the speed with which he forgets and is forgotten. Lasting fame is a mirage. Many of us would have great difficulty in naming our great-grandparents. And fewer, perhaps, could name the last four vice-presidents of the United States. In our self-importance, we think that the world can't get on without us; yet we die and are quickly forgotten, and life on the planet goes on as usual.

So much for Solomon's conclusions. Now he is going to retrace for us the pilgrimage he made in search of the summum bonum—the greatest good in life. He reminds us (v. 12) that he was king over Israel in Jerusalem, with all that implies of wealth, status, and ability.

When Solomon says "I . . . was king" (KJV), he does not mean that his reign had ended. He was king and still is king (v. 1).

In verse 13, Solomon begins his search for happiness "under the sun." First, he decides to travel the intellectual route. He thinks he might be happy if he could just acquire enough knowledge. So he applies himself to get the most comprehensive education possible. He devotes himself to research and exploration, synthesis and analysis, induction and deduction. But he soon becomes disenchanted with learning as an end in itself. In fact, he says that it is an unhappy business with which God allows men to occupy themselves—this deep inner drive to find out the meaning of life.

He reminds me of a contemporary sage who reached a similar conclusion. Malcolm Muggeridge wrote in *Jesus Rediscovered:*

Education, the great mumbo-jumbo and fraud of the ages, purports to equip us to live, and is prescribed as a universal remedy for everything from juvenile delinquency to premature senility. For the most part, it only serves to enlarge stupidity, inflate conceit, enhance credulity and put those subjected to it at the mercy of brainwashers with printing presses, radio and television at their disposal.[4]

Recently someone painted this telling graffiti in bold, black letters on the wall of a university library: APATHY RULES. Someone had found what Solomon had learned centuries earlier—that education is not the sure road to fulfillment, but that, taken by itself, it can be a bore.

This does not mean that intellectual pursuit cannot play an important role in life. There is a place for it, but that place is at the feet of Christ. It should not be an end in itself but a means of glorifying Him.

The reference to God in this verse must not be equated with deep personal faith. The name of God is what W. J. Erdman calls His natural name—Elohim.[5] As I mentioned in the introduction, this name presents Him as the almighty One who created the universe. But nowhere in this book does Solomon acknowledge Him as the covenant-keeping Jehovah who shows redeeming grace to those who put their trust in Him.

There can be no doubt that Solomon got the best education that was available in Israel at that time. This is apparent from his unblushing claim to have seen everything that is done under the sun (v. 14). What this means is that he became highly knowledgeable in the sciences, philosophy, history, the fine arts, the social sciences, literature, religion, psychology, ethics, languages, and other fields of human learning.

But an alphabet of degrees after his name and a room papered with diplomas didn't give him what he was seeking. On the contrary, he concluded that it was all a chase after something as elusive as the wind.

He was frustrated to discover that book learning doesn't solve all the puzzles of life. There are crooked things that cannot be straightened and missing things that cannot be counted (v. 15). Robert Laurin has observed, "Life is full of paradoxes and anomalies that cannot be solved; and contrariwise, it is empty of so much that could give it meaning and value."[6]

Man can fly to the moon, but the flight of a bee defies all known laws of aerodynamics. Scientists have delved into the secrets of the atom, but they cannot harness lightning or store its power. Diseases such as polio and tuberculosis have been controlled, but the common cold is still unconquered.

After he had won all his academic laurels, Solomon took personal inventory (v. 16). He could boast that he had more wisdom than all those who had ruled in Jerusalem before him (1 Ki 4:29-31; 2 Ch 1:12). His mind had absorbed an enormous fund of knowledge. And he had wisdom as well; he knew how to apply his knowledge to the practical, everyday affairs of life, to make sound judgments, and to deal judiciously with others.

In verse 17, Solomon reminisced about how he had disciplined himself to acquire wisdom on the one hand, and to learn about madness and folly on the other. In other words, he explored both extremes of human behavior, just in case the true meaning of life was found in either or in both. He ran the gamut of life's experiences, but his disconsolate conclusion was that it was all a striving after wind.

Centuries later, a young fellow named Henry Martyn sought and won top honors at Cambridge University. Yet in the hour of his academic triumph, he said, "I was surprised to find I had grasped a shadow." It was a blessed disillusionment for, as J. W. Jowett noted, "His eyes were now lifted far above scholastic prizes to the all-satisfying prize of the high calling of God in Christ Jesus our Lord."

If intellectualism is the key to meaning in life, then our college campuses would be Camelots of peace and contentment. But they are not. Rather they are cauldrons of ferment and unrest. The timeworn caricature of a college student, swathing his head in a turkish towel and washing down aspirin with huge mugs of coffee, fits in well with Solomon's conclusion in verse 18, "In much wisdom there is much grief, and increasing knowledge results in increasing pain." In other words, "The wiser you are the more worries you have; the more you know, the more it hurts." According to this, there is some truth to the adages, "Ignorance is bliss," and "What you don't know won't hurt you."

2

The Pointless Pursuit of Pleasure and Prestige

Having failed to find fulfillment in intellectual pursuit, Solomon turns in chapter 2 to the pursuit of pleasure (v. 1). *It seems reasonable that one would be happy if one could just enjoy enough pleasure,* he thought. Pleasure, by definition, means the enjoyable sensations that come from the gratification of personal desires. So he decided that he would live it up, that he would try to experience every stimulation of the senses known to man. He would drink the cup of fun to the full, and then, at last, his heart would ask no more.

But the search ended in failure. He concludes that pleasures under the sun are empty. His disappointment is echoed in the verse:

> I tried the broken cisterns, Lord,
> But ah, the waters failed.
> E'en as I stooped to drink they fled
> And mocked me as I wailed.[1]
> B.E.

Does this mean that God is opposed to His people having pleasure? Not at all. In fact the reverse is true. God wants His people to have a good life. But He wants us to realize that

21

this world cannot afford true pleasure. It can only be found above the sun. In His "presence is fulness of joy;" at His "right hand there are pleasures for evermore" (Ps 16:11, KJV). In that sense, God is the greatest hedonist or pleasure lover of all.

The big lie promulgated by the movies, TV, and the advertising media is that man can make his own heaven down here without God. But Solomon learned that all this world can offer are cesspools and cisterns, whereas God offers the fountain of life.

As he thinks back on all the empty laughter (v. 2), he sees that it was mad, and all his good times actually accomplished nothing. And so it is. Behind all the laughing there is sorrow, and those who try to entertain others are often in great need of personal help.

Billy Graham tells in *The Secret of Happiness* of the disturbed patient who consulted a psychiatrist for help. He was suffering from deep depression. Nothing he had tried could help. He woke up discouraged and blue, and the condition worsened as the day progressed. Now he was desperate; he couldn't go on this way.

Before he left the office, the psychiatrist told him about a show in one of the local theaters. It featured an Italian clown who had the audience convulsed with laughter night after night. The doctor recommended that his patient attend the show, that it would be excellent therapy to laugh for a couple of hours and forget his troubles. Just go and see the Italian clown!

With a hangdog expression, the patient muttered, "I am that clown." He too could say of laughter, "It is mad," and of pleasure, "What use is it?"

How often in life we look at others and imagine that they have no problems, no hang-ups, no needs. But E. A. Robinson shatters the illusion in his poem, "Richard Cory."

> Whenever Richard Cory went down town,
> We people on the pavement looked at him:

> He was a gentleman from sole to crown,
> Clean favored, and imperially slim.
>
> And he was always quietly arrayed,
> And he was always human when he talked;
> But still he fluttered pulses when he said,
> "Good morning," and he glittered when he walked.
>
> And he was rich—yes, richer than a king—
> And admirably schooled in every grace;
> In fine, we thought that he was everything
> To make us wish that we were in his place.
>
> So on we worked, and waited for the light,
> And went without the meat, and cursed the bread;
> And Richard Cory, one calm summer night,
> Went home and put a bullet through his head.[2]

Next Solomon, the Old Testament prodigal, turns to wine. He would become a connoisseur of the choicest vintages. Perhaps if he could experience the most exquisite taste sensations, his whole being would relax satisfied.

He was wise enough to place a bound on his Epicureanism. It is expressed in the words, "My mind was guiding me wisely" (v. 3). In other words, he would not abandon himself to intemperance or drunkenness. There was no thought of his becoming addicted to strong drink. And nowhere in his search for reality did he suggest his becoming hooked on drugs. He was too wise for that.

Another thing he tried was folly, that is, harmless and enjoyable forms of nonsense. Just in case wisdom didn't hold the answer, he decided to explore its opposite. Sometimes people who are clods seem to be happier than those who are very clever. So he didn't want to leave that stone unturned. He turned his attention to trivia, indulgence, and amusement. It was a desperate ploy to discover the best way for man to occupy himself during his few fleeting days under the sun. But he didn't find the answer there.

So Solomon, according to verses 4 and 5, decided to

embark on a vast real-estate program. If education, pleasure, wine, or folly didn't hold the key, then surely possessions did. He built luxurious houses and planted vineyards by the acre. From what we know of Solomon's building programs, we can be sure that he spared no expense.

He built enormous estates with parks and gardens—literal paradises. Orchards with all kinds of fruit trees punctuated the landscape. It's easy to imagine him taking his friends on guided tours and having his ego inflated by their expressions of awe and enthusiasm.

Probably none of his guests had the courage to say to him what Samuel Johnson said to a millionaire who was taking a similar ego trip. After seeing all the luxury and magnificence, Johnson remarked, ''These are the things that make it hard for a man to die.''

The world still has its share of deluded millionaires, like the king in Andersen's tale, *The Emperor's Clothes*. This king went on parade in what he wanted to believe were stunningly beautiful clothes, but even a little child could see that he was stark naked.

Such vast estates needed irrigation during the hot, dry summers. So Solomon constructed aqueducts, lakes, and ponds, with all the necessary canals, ditches, and ducts to transport the water (v. 6).

If the accumulation of possessions could guarantee peace and happiness, then he had arrived. But like the rest of us, he had to learn that true pleasure comes from noble renunciations rather than from frenzied accumulations. He was spending his money on that which is not bread and his labor for that which does not satisfy (Is 55:2).

Battalions of servants were needed to operate and maintain the king's grandiose estates, so he hired male and female slaves (v. 7). What is more, he had slaves that were born in his house—an exceptionally important status symbol in the culture of that time.

To Solomon, as to most men, one aspect of greatness lay in

being served. To sit at the table was greater than to serve. A greater than Solomon came into the world as a Slave of slaves and showed us that true greatness in His Kingdom lies in servanthood (Mk 10:43-45; Lk 9:24-27).

The largest herds and flocks ever owned by any resident of Jerusalem grazed in the pastures of Solomon's ranches. If prestige was the key to a happy life, then he held the key. But it wasn't, and he didn't. Someone has said, "I asked for all things that I might enjoy life; I was given life that I might enjoy all things."

And what shall we say about his financial resources! He had gold and silver in abundance and the treasure of kings and provinces. This may mean the taxes which he collected from those under him or wealth taken from conquered territories, or it may refer to objets d'art which were presented to him by visiting dignitaries such as the Queen of Sheba.

He tried music (v. 8). Music has power to charm, they say. So he assembled the finest singing talent, both men and women. The Jerusalem news probably carried rave reviews of all the public concerts. But of course the king had private performances too—dinner music, chamber ensembles—you name it. Yet I think his disappointment was well expressed by Samuel Johnson in *The History of Rasselas, The Prince of Abyssinia:*

> "I likewise can call the lutanist and the singer, but the sounds that pleased me yesterday weary me today, and will grow yet more wearisome tomorrow. I can discover within me no power of perception which is not glutted with its proper pleasure, yet I do not feel myself delighted. Man has surely some latent sense for which this place affords no gratification, or he has some desires distinct from sense which must be satisfied before he can be happy."[3]

And he tried sex. Not just wine (v. 3) and song (v. 8) but women as well. Wine, women, and song! "The pleasures of men—many concubines" (v. 8). The Bible tells us factually though not approvingly that Solomon had 700 wives and 300 concubines (1 Ki 11:3). And did he suppose this was the way to happiness? Just think of all the jealousy, gossip, and backbiting possible in such a harem.

And yet the delusion persists in our own sick society that sex is a highway to happiness and fulfillment. Within the God-appointed bounds of monogamous marriage, that can be true. But the abuse of sex leads only to misery and self-destruction.

A victim of today's sex-obsession felt afterward that she had been cheated. She wrote: "I guess I wanted sex to be some psychedelic jackpot that made the whole world light up like a pinball machine, but when it was all over I felt I had been shortchanged. I remember thinking, 'Is that all there is? Is that all there *really* is?' "[4]

So Solomon became Mr. Big (v. 9). He had the satisfaction of outclimbing all his predecessors on the prestige ladder —for whatever that satisfaction is worth. And his natural wisdom was still with him after all his experiments and excursions. He hadn't lost his head.

In his search for satisfaction, he had placed no limits on his expenditures. If he saw something he wanted, he bought it (v. 10). If he thought he'd enjoy some pleasure, he treated himself to it. He found a certain sense of gratification in this ceaseless round of getting things and doing things. This fleeting joy was all the reward he got for his exertions in pursuing pleasure and possessions.

Then he took stock of all that he had done, and of all the energy he had expended (v. 11), and what was the result? It was all emptiness and futility, a striving after wind. He hadn't found lasting satisfaction under the sun. He found, like Luther, that "the empire of the whole world is but a crust to be thrown to a dog." He was bored by it all.

Ralph Barton, a top cartoonist, was bored too. He wrote: "I have had few difficulties, many friends, great successes. I have gone from wife to wife, from house to house, and have visited great countries of the world. But I am fed up with devices to fill up twenty four hours of the day."[5]

The failure of pleasure and possessions to fill the heart of man was further illustrated by a fictional character who only had to wish for something and he got it instantly. "He wanted a house and there it was with servants at the door; he wanted a Cadillac, and there it was with chauffeur. He was elated at the beginning, but it soon began to pall on him. He said to an attendant, 'I want to get out of this. I want to create something, to suffer something. I would rather be in hell than here.' And the attendant answered, 'Where do you think you are?' "[6]

That is where our contemporary society is—in a hell of materialism, trying to satisfy the human heart with things that cannot bring lasting enjoyment.

Because of the disheartening outcome of all his research, Solomon began to wonder whether it's better to be a wise man or a fool (v. 12). He decided to look into the matter. Since life is such a chase after bubbles, does the man who lives prudently have any advantage over the one who goes to the other extreme, having a good time in madness and folly?

Being the king, and a wise and wealthy one at that, he was in a good position to find out. If he couldn't find out, what chance did anyone succeeding him have? Anyone coming after the king could scarcely discover any new light on the subject.

His general conclusion was that wisdom is better than folly in the same way and to the same degree that light excels darkness (v. 13). The wise man walks in the light and can see the dangers in the way. The fool, on the other hand, gropes along in darkness and falls into every ditch and trap.

But even granting that advantage—that the wise man has eyes to see where he is going—what final difference does it make? They both die eventually and no amount of wisdom can delay or cancel that appointment. It is the lot of all (v. 14).

In verse 15, when Solomon realized that the same fate was awaiting him as awaited the fool, he wondered why he had put such a premium on wisdom all his life. The only redeeming feature of wisdom is that it sheds light on the way. Apart from that, it is no better. And so the pursuit of wisdom is also a great waste of effort.

He continues this idea into verses 16 and 17. After the funeral, both the wise man and the fool are quickly forgotten. Within a generation or two, it is as if they had never lived. The names and faces that seem so important today will fade into oblivion. As far as lasting fame is concerned, the wise man is no better off than the fool.

The chilling realization that fame is ephemeral and that man is quickly forgotten made Solomon hate life. Instead of finding satisfaction and fulfillment in human activity under the sun, he found only grief. It troubled him to realize that everything was futile and a striving after wind.

A former athlete who had achieved fame said, "The greatest thrill of my life was when I first scored the decisive goal in a big game and heard the roar of the cheering crowds. But in the quiet of my room that same night, a sense of the futility of it swept over me. After all, what was it worth? Was there nothing better to live for than to score goals? Such thoughts were the beginning of my search for satisfaction. I knew in my heart that no one could meet my need but God Himself. Soon after, I found in Christ what I could never find in the world."[7]

One of the greatest injustices that bothered Solomon was that he would not be permitted to enjoy the wealth which he had accumulated (v. 18). C. E. Stuart wrote, "Death is a worm at the root of the tree of pleasure. It mars pleasure, it chills enjoyment, for it cuts off man just when he would sit down after years of toil to reap the fruit of his labor." And he has to leave it all to his heir.

The galling thing is that the heir may not be a wise man (v. 19). He may be a spendthrift, a stupid fellow, a playboy, a loafer, but he will inherit the estate nevertheless. He will preside over the dissipation of a fortune for which he neither labored nor planned.

This really nettled Solomon. Perhaps he had a premonition that it would happen in his own family. Perhaps Solomon foresaw that his son, Rehoboam, would squander by his folly all that he had worked so hard to accumulate. History tells us that Rehoboam did just that. By refusing to listen to his older counselors, he precipitated the division of the kingdom. When the Egyptians invaded Judah, he bought them off by giving them the temple treasures. "The shields of gold went to swell the coffers of Egypt, and Rehoboam had to substitute shields of brass in their stead" (see 2 Ch 12:9-10).

The prospect of having to leave his life's work and wealth to an unworthy successor plunged the Preacher into gloom and depression (v. 20). It seemed so senseless and incongruous. It made him feel that all his efforts were for nothing.

The whole idea distressed him (v. 21), that a man who builds up financial resources through wise investments, shrewd business decisions, and skillful moves is forced at death to leave it to someone who never did a lick of work for it or expended an ounce of worry. What is this but an absurdity and a great calamity?

In spite of Solomon's finding, parents throughout the world still spend the best part of their lives accumulating wealth that will be left to their children. They altruistically describe it as their moral obligation. But Jamieson, Fausset, and Brown suggest, "Selfishness is mostly at the root of worldly parents' alleged providence for their children."[8] Their first thought is to provide luxuriously for their own old age. They are thinking primarily of themselves. That their children inherit what is left is only the result of the parents' death and the laws of inheritance.

From the Christian perspective, there is no reason for parents to work, scrimp, save, and sacrifice in order to leave money to their children. The best heritage to bequeath is spiritual, not financial. Money left in wills has often caused serious jealousy and disunity in otherwise happy and compatible families. Children have been ruined spiritually and morally by suddenly becoming inheritors of large bequests. Other evils almost inevitably follow.

The spiritual approach is to put our money to work for God now and not to leave it to children who are sometimes unworthy, ungrateful, and even unsaved. Martin Luther felt he could trust his family to God as he had trusted himself. In his last will and testament he wrote:

> Lord God, I thank Thee, for thou hast been pleased to make me a poor and indigent man upon earth. I have neither house nor land nor money to leave behind me. Thou hast given me wife and children, whom I now restore to Thee. Lord, nourish, teach and preserve them, as Thou hast me.

Solomon concludes that man has nothing of enduring value as a result of all his labor and heartache under the sun (v. 22). He strives, he plods, he frets and fumes—but for what? What difference does it all make five minutes after he dies?

Apart from revelation, we would come to the same conclusion. But we know from God's Word that our lives can be lived for God and for eternity. We know that all that is done for Him will be rewarded. Our labor is not in vain in the Lord (1 Co 15:58).

For the man who has no hope beyond the grave, however, it is true that his days are filled with pain and vexatious work, and his nights with tossing and turning (v. 23). Life is a king-sized frustration, filled with worry and heartache.

This being the case, a logical philosophy of life for the man whose whole existence is under the sun is to find enjoyment in eating, drinking, and in his daily work (v. 24). The Preacher is not advocating gluttony and drunkenness but rather finding pleasure wherever possible in the common things of life. Even this is from the hand of God—that men should enjoy the normal mercies of life, the taste of good food, the refreshment of table beverages, and the satisfaction that comes from honest work. Man does not have the power of enjoyment unless it is given to him by God.

A later preacher, the apostle Paul, confirmed Solomon's outlook. He said that if there is no resurrection of the dead then the best policy would be, "Let us eat and drink; for tomorrow we die" (1 Co 15:32, KJV).

Going back to Solomon's observations in Ecclesiastes 2:24, he adds that the ability to eat and find enjoyment in other ways comes from God. Without Him, we cannot enjoy the most ordinary pleasures. We depend on Him for food, appetite, digestion, sight, hearing, smell, memory, health, sanity, and all that makes for normal, pleasurable experiences. In verse 25, he adds that he was able to enjoy all these things more than anyone.

John D. Rockefeller had an income of about a million dollars a week, yet all his doctors allowed him to eat cost only a few cents. One of his biographers said that he lived on a diet that a pauper would have despised. "Now less than a hundred pounds in weight, he sampled everything (at breakfast): a drop of coffee, a spoonful of cereal, a forkful of egg, and a bit of chop the size of a pea."[9] He was the richest man in the world but did not have the ability to enjoy his food.

Finally (v. 26), the Preacher felt that he observed a general principle in life that God rewards righteousness and punishes sin. To the man who pleases Him, He gives wisdom, knowledge, and joy. But to the habitual sinner, He gives the burden of hard work, accumulating and piling up, only to see it taken over by someone who strikes God's fancy. What could be more fruitless and defeating than that?

3

A Time for Everything

As a research student of life and of human behavior, it appeared to Solomon that there is a predetermined season for everything and a fixed time for every happening (3:1). This means that God has programmed every activity into a gigantic computer, and, as the Spanish say, *"Que sera, sera"*: What will be, will be! It also means that history is filled with cyclical patterns, and these recur with unchangeable regularity. So man is locked into a pattern of behavior which is determined by certain inflexible laws or principles. He is a slave to fatalism's clock and calendar.

In the verses that follow, the Preacher enumerates twenty-eight activities which are probably intended to symbolize the whole round of life. This is suggested by the number twenty-eight, which is the number of the world (four) multiplied by the number of completeness (seven).

The list is made up of opposites. Fourteen are positives and fourteen negatives. In some ways, they seem to cancel out each other so that the net result is zero.

There is a time to be born (v. 2). The person himself has no control over this, and even the parents must wait out the nine months which form the normal birth cycle.

And there is a time to die. Man's allotted span is seventy years, according to Psalm 90:10, but even apart from that, it seems that death is a predetermined appointment that must be kept.

It is true that God foreknows the terminus of our life on earth, but for the Christian this is neither morbid nor fatalistic. We know that we are immortal until our work is done. And though death is a possibility, it is not a certainty. The blessed hope of Christ's return inspires the believer to look for the Saviour rather than the mortician.

"A time to plant, and a time to uproot what is planted." With these words, Solomon seems to cover the entire field of agriculture, linked closely as it is with the seasons of the year (Gen 8:22). Failure to observe these seasons in planting and harvesting can only spell disaster.

"A time to kill, and a time to heal" (v. 3, KJV). Bible commentators go to great lengths to explain that this cannot refer to murder but only to warfare, capital punishment, or self-defense. But we must remember that Solomon's observations were based on his knowledge under the sun. Without divine revelation, it seemed to him that life was either a slaughterhouse or a hospital, a battlefield or a first-aid station.

"A time to tear down, and a time to build up." First the wrecking crew appears to demolish buildings that are outdated and no longer serviceable, then the builders move in to erect modern complexes and rehabilitate the area of blight.

"A time to weep, and a time to laugh" (v. 4, KJV). Life seems to alternate between tragedy and comedy. Now it wears the black mask of the tragedian, then the painted face of the clown.

"A time to mourn, and a time to dance." The funeral procession passes by with its mourners wailing in grief. But before long, these same people are dancing at a wedding reception, quickly removed from their recent sorrow.

"A time to cast away stones, and a time to gather stones together" (v. 5, KJV). Taken at face value, this means that there is a time to clear land for cultivation (Is 5:2), then to gather the stones for building houses, walls, or other projects. If we take the words figuratively, as most modern commentators do, there may be a reference to the marriage act. Thus, *Today's English Version* paraphrases, "The time for having sex and the time for not having it."

"A time to embrace, and a time to shun embracing." In the realm of the affections, there is a time for involvement and a time for withdrawal. There is a time when love is pure and a time when it is illicit.

"A time to seek, and a time to lose" (v. 6, JND). This makes us think of business cycles with their fluctuating profits and losses. First the markets are bullish with income soaring. Then they become bearish, and companies find themselves in the red.

"A time to keep, and a time to throw away." Most housewives are familiar with this curious pattern. For months or even years, they stash things away in closets, basements, and attics. Then in a burst of housecleaning zeal, they clear them out and call some local charity to cart the gathered items away.

"A time to rend, and a time to sew" (v. 7, KJV). Could Solomon have been thinking of the constant changes in clothing fashions? Some noted fashion designer dictates a new trend, and all over the world, hems are let out or shortened. Today the fashions are daring and attention getting. Tomorrow they revert to the quaint styles of grandmother's day.

"A time to be silent, and a time to speak." The time to keep silence is when we are criticized unjustly, when we are tempted to criticize others, or to say things that are untrue, unkind, or unedifying. Because Moses spoke unadvisedly with his lips, he was barred from entering the promised land (Num 20:10; Ps 106:33).

The time to speak is when some great principle or cause is at stake. Mordecai advised Esther that the time had come for her to speak (Est 4:13-14). And he could have added, with Dante, "The hottest places in hell are reserved for those who remain neutral in a time of great moral crisis."

"A time to love, and a time to hate" (v. 8, KJV). We must not try to force these words into a Christian context. Solomon was not speaking as a Christian but as a man of the world. It seemed to him that human behavior fluctuated between periods of love and periods of hate.

"A time for war, and a time for peace." What is history if it is not the record of cruel, mindless wars, interspersed with short terms of peace?

The question lingering in Solomon's mind was, What lasting gain has a worker for all his toil? (v. 9). For every constructive activity there is a destructive one. For every plus a minus. The fourteen positive works are cancelled out by fourteen negatives. So the mathematical formula of life is fourteen minus fourteen equals zero. Man has nothing but a zero at the end of it all.

Solomon had conducted an exhaustive survey of all the activities, employments, and pursuits that God has given to man to occupy his time (v. 10). He has just given us a catalog of these in verses 2-8.

He concluded that God has made everything beautiful in its time (v. 11), or, better, that there is an appropriate time for each activity. He is not so much thinking here of the beauty of God's creation as the fact that every action has its own designated time, and that in its time it is eminently fitting.

God also has put eternity in man's mind. Though living in a world of time, man has intimations of eternity. Instinctively he thinks of "forever," and though he cannot understand the concept, he realizes that beyond this life there is the possibility of a shoreless ocean of time.

Yet God's works and ways are inscrutable to man. There is no way in which we can solve the riddle of creation, providence, or the consummation of the universe, apart from revelation. In spite of the enormous advances of human

knowledge, we still see through a glass darkly. Very often we
have to confess with a sigh, "How little we know of Him!"

Because man's life is governed by certain inexorable laws
and because all his activities seem to leave him where he
started, Solomon decides that the best policy is to be happy
and enjoy life as much as possible (v. 12).

He did not mean that life should be an orgy of drunkenness, dissipation, and debauchery, but that God's best for
man is that he should enjoy his food and drink and find what
pleasure he can in his daily work (v. 13). It is a low view of
life, and completely sub-Christian in its outlook, but we must
continually remember that Solomon's viewpoint here was
thoroughly earthbound.

He did accurately perceive that God's decrees are immutable (v. 14). What God has decided will stand and man
cannot alter it, either by addition or subtraction. It is foolish
for creatures to fight against the arrangements of their
Creator. Much better to respect Him and submit to His
control.

Current events are merely a replay of what has happened
previously, and nothing will happen in the future but what
has already taken place (v. 15). God arranges everything on a
recurring basis so that things will happen over and over
again. He brings back again what is past and thus history
repeats itself. The expression "God requireth that which is
past" (KJV) is often used to press home the fact that past
sins must be accounted for by unbelievers. While this is true,
it is hardly the force of this passage. Here God is rather seen
as recalling past events to form another cycle of history.
T. S. Eliot, in *The Four Quartets,* confirms Solomon's sentiments:

> And what is there to conquer . . . has already
>   been discovered
> Once or twice or several times . . .
> There is only the fight to recover what has been lost
> And found and lost again and again.[1]

Among other things that pained the Preacher were injustice and corruption (v. 16). He found crookedness in the law courts where justice should be dispensed and dishonesty in government circles where righteousness should be practiced. These inequalities of life led him to believe that there has to be a time when God will judge men, when the wrongs of earth will be made right (v. 17). Solomon does not say explicitly that this will be in the next life, but it is a foregone conclusion since so many inequities are unrequited in this world. His conclusion mirrors a common emotion in the hearts of righteous people. Decency and fairness demand a time when accounts are settled and when the right is vindicated.

In the closing verses of chapter 3, the Preacher turns to the subject of death, and sees it as the grim spoilsport, ending all man's best ambitions, endeavors, and pleasures (v. 18). He views it exactly as we would if we did not have the Bible to enlighten us.

Notice that he introduces his views with the words, *I said to myself*. It is not a question of what God revealed to him but of what he concluded in his own mind. It is his own reasoning under the sun. Therefore, this is not a passage from which we can build an adequate doctrine of death and the hereafter. And yet this is precisely what many of the false cults have done. They use these verses to support their erroneous teachings of soul-sleep and the annihilation of the wicked dead. Actually a careful study of the passage will show that Solomon was not advocating either of these views.

Basically what he is saying is that God is testing man through his short life on earth to show him how frail and transient he is—just like the animals. But is he saying that man is no better than an animal?

No, the point is not that man is a beast, but that in *one respect*, he has no advantage over a beast. As death comes to an animal, so it comes to man (v. 19). All have one breath, and at the time of death, that breath is cut off. So life is as empty for man as for the lower orders of creation.

All share a common end in the grave (v. 20). They are both going to the same place—the dust. They both came from it; they will both go back to it. Of course, this assumes that the body is all there is to human life. But we know that this is not true. The body is only the tent in which the person lives. But Solomon could not be expected to know the full truth of the future state.

Solomon's ignorance as to what happens at the time of death is evident from his question, "Who knows that the breath of man ascends upward and the breath of the beast descends downward to the earth?" (v. 21). This must not be taken as a doctrinal fact. It is human questioning, not divine certainty.

From the New Testament, we know that the spirit and soul of the believer go to be with Christ at the time of death (2 Co 5:8; Phil 1:23), and his body goes to the grave (Ac 8:2). The spirit and soul of the unbeliever goes to hades, and his body goes to the grave (Lk 16:22b-23). When Christ comes into the air, the bodies of those who have died in faith will be raised in glorified form and reunited with the spirit and soul (Phil 3:20-21; 1 Th 4:16-17). The bodies of the unbelieving dead will be raised at the Great White Throne Judgment, reunited with the spirit and soul, then cast into the lake of fire (Rev 20:12-14).

Strictly speaking, animals have body and soul but no spirit. Nothing is said in the Bible concerning life after death for animals.

From what he knew about death, and also from what he didn't know, Solomon figures that the best thing a man can do is enjoy his daily activities (v. 22). That, after all, is his lot in life, and he might as well cooperate with the inevitable. He should find satisfaction in accepting what cannot be changed. But above all, he should enjoy life as it comes to him, because no one can tell him what is going to happen on earth after he has passed on.

4

Life Is Not Fair

Robert Burns said, "Man's inhumanity to man makes countless thousands mourn!" Sensitive hearts in every age have been grieved to see the oppressions that are carried out by men against their fellowmen. It tormented Solomon also. In Ecclesiastes 4:1, he was grieved to see the tears of the oppressed, the power of their oppressors, and the failure of anyone to defend the downtrodden. Power was on the side of the oppressors, and no one dared to defy that power. From this vantage point, it seemed that "Truth [was] forever on the scaffold, Wrong forever on the throne." He could not see that "behind the dim unknown, standeth God within the shadow, keeping watch above His own."[1]

So in his dejection, he concluded that the dead are better off than the living (v. 2). To him, death provided welcome escape from all the persecutions and cruelties of this life. He was not concerned at the moment with the deeper implications of death—that a person who dies in unbelief is doomed to more severe suffering than the worst oppression on earth. For him the question was not, Is there life after death? but rather, Is there life after birth?

Solomon's cynicism touched bottom with the observation that though the dead are better off than the living, the unborn are still more enviable (v. 3). They have never lived to be driven mad by oppressions under the sun. They have never had to endure "that ghastly mockery of happiness called life."

There was something else that drove him up the wall—the fact that human activity and skill are motivated by the desire to outdo one's neighbor (v. 4). He saw that the wheel of life was propelled by the competitive spirit. The desire to have a better car, a faster boat, a more luxurious home—it all seemed so empty and unworthy of men created in God's image and after His likeness.

When Michelangelo and Raphael were commissioned to use their artistic talents for the adornment of the Vatican, a deep spirit of rivalry broke out between them. "Although each had a different job to do, they became so jealous that at last they would not even speak to one another."[2] Some are more adept at concealing their envy than these geniuses were, but this same attitude of rivalry is at the bottom of much contemporary activity.

A modern cynic has written, "I've tried everything that life has to offer, but all I see is one guy trying to outdo another in a futile attempt at happiness."[3]

In contrast to those whose motive and reward is envy is the fool—the dull, stupid sluggard (v. 5). He folds his hands and lives off what little food he can get without much exertion. Perhaps he is wiser than his neighbors who are driven relentlessly on by their envy and covetousness.

While those around him are working themselves into a frenzy of competition, the fool's sentiments are "One hand full of rest is better than two fists full of labor and striving after wind" (v. 6). Or as H. C. Leupold paraphrases it, "Rather would I have my ease, though I possess but little, than acquire more and have all the vexation that goes with it."

There was another kind of folly which blew the Preacher's mind. It was the mindless craze of the man who is alone, to keep working and accumulating wealth (vv. 7-8). He has no son, no brother, no close relatives. He already has more money than he will ever need. Yet he wears himself out day after day and denies himself the simple amenities of life. It never occurs to him to ask for whom he is working so hard and living so frugally. Charles Bridges in his exposition comments, "The miser—how well he deserves the name—the wretched slave of mammon, grown old as a toiling, scraping, griping drudge!" His name is miser and as his name, so is he—miserable. What an empty, wretched way to live, thought Solomon!

Surely Samuel Johnson was right when he said, "the lust for gold, unfeeling and remorseless, is the last corruption of degenerate man."

The solitariness of the miser leads Solomon to point out the advantages of fellowship and partnership (v. 9). He uses four illustrations to press home his thesis. First of all, two workers are better than one, because by cooperation they can produce more efficiently.

Also if there is an accident on the job, one can help the other (v. 10). But pity the man who falls off the ladder when he is alone. There is no one around to call for help.

Two in a bed on a cold night are better than one because they help to keep each other warm (v. 11). I suppose we could shoot holes in his argument by mentioning the annoyance caused by the partner who has cold feet or who hogs the covers, or the controlled heat that comes from an electric blanket. But the point remains that there are pleasures and benefits from social intercourse and friendship that are unknowable to the one who lives in isolation.

The third illustration has to do with protection against attack (v. 12). A thief can often overpower one victim, but two can usually resist the intruder successfully.

Finally, a rope made with three cords is stronger than one with only one or even two strands. In fact, three strands twisted together are more than three times as strong as three separate strands.

The follies and vanities of life are not confined to the peons; they are even found in the palaces of kings (vv. 13-16). Solomon describes a king who overcame poverty and a prison record in his rise to the throne; yet now when he is old, he is intractable. He will not listen to his advisers. It would be better to have a young man who is teachable, even though poor, to reign in his place. Solomon thought about all the people who are subjects of the king and about the young man who is second in the chain of command—the heir apparent. Multitudes flock to his banner. They are tired of the old king and want a change, hoping for a better administration. But, even the ones who will come later will not be happy with him (v. 16).

This fickleness and craving for novelty made Solomon realize that even the world's highest honors are empty. They too are like chasing the wind.

5

Advice to the Religious
and the Rich

Man is instinctively religious, but that is not necessarily good. In fact, it may be positively bad. His very religiosity may hide from him his need of salvation as a free gift of God's grace. In addition, man's own religion may be nothing more than a charade, an outward show without inward reality. Vanity may seep into religious life just as much as in any other sphere, maybe even more so. So, in chapter 5, Solomon lays down some advice to guard against formalism and externalism in dealing with the Creator.

First, he advises people to watch their steps when they go into the house of God (v. 1). While this may refer to reverence in general, here it is explained to mean being more ready to learn than to engage in a lot of rash talk. Rash promises are the sacrifice of fools. Unthinking people make them without considering that it is sinful.

Worshipers should avoid recklessness in prayers, promises, or in professions of devotion to God (v. 2). The presence of the Almighty is no place for precipitate or compulsive talking. The fact that God is infinitely high above man, as heaven is high above the earth, should teach man to curb his speech when drawing near to Him.

Just as a hyperactive mind often produces wild dreams, so a hyperactive mouth produces a torrent of foolish words, even in a prayer (v. 3). Alexander Pope wrote that "Words are like leaves, and where they most abound, much fruit of sense beneath is rarely found."

I don't suppose Solomon intended verse 3 to be a full, scientific explanation of the origin of dreams; he was merely pointing out what seemed to him to be a connection between the whirring wheels of his mind during the day and the restless dreams that often followed at night.

In the matter of vows to God, simple honesty demands that they be paid promptly (v. 4). God has no use for the dolt who talks up a storm then fails to deliver. So the word is "pay what you vow."

If you don't intend to pay, don't make a vow in the first place (v. 5).

How well the Preacher knew man's propensity to strike a bargain with God when caught in a tight, desperate situation: "Lord, if you get me out of this, I'll serve you forever." But then the tendency is to forget quickly when the crisis is past.

Even in moments of spiritual exhilaration, it is easy to make a vow of dedication, or celibacy, or poverty, or the like. God has never required such vows of His people. In many cases, such as in the matter of celibacy, it would be better not to make them anyway. But where they are made, they should be kept. Certainly the marriage vow is ratified in heaven and cannot be broken without costly consequences. Vows made before conversion should be kept, except in those cases where they violate the Word of God.

So the general rule is not to let your mouth lead you into sin through shattered vows (v. 6). And don't try to excuse yourself before God's messenger by saying it was a mistake and that you didn't really mean it. Or don't think that the mechanical offering of a sacrifice before Him will atone for careless breaking of vows.

The "messenger" may refer to the priest, since broken vows were to be confessed before him (Lev 5:4-6). But this presupposes a knowledge of the Mosaic law, whereas Solomon is speaking here apart from revealed religion. So perhaps we are safer to understand him as meaning anyone who serves as a representative of God.

The basic thought is that God is exceedingly displeased by insincerity of speech. Why then say things that are certain to anger Him? This will inevitably cause Him to obstruct, defeat, and frustrate everything you try to do.

Just as there is tremendous unreality in a multitude of dreams, so in words spoken unadvisedly there is futility and ruin (v. 7). The thing to do, says Solomon, is to fear God. However, he does not mean the loving trust of Jehovah but the actual fear of incurring the displeasure of the Almighty. G. C. Morgan reminds us that this is the fear of a slave, not a son. Unless we see this, we give Solomon credit for a greater burst of spiritual insight than is intended here.

Next Solomon reverts to the subject of oppression of the poor and perversion of justice (v. 8). He counsels against complete despair, if we see these evils in a province. After all, there are chains of command in government, and those in the higher echelons watch their subordinates with an eagle eye.

But do they really? Too often the system of checks and balances breaks down, and every level of officialdom receives its share of the graft and payola.

The only satisfaction that righteous people have is in knowing that God is higher than the highest authorities, and He will see that all accounts are settled some day. But it is doubtful if Solomon refers to this here.

To me, verse 9 is the most obscure verse in the book of Ecclesiastes. The reason is that the original Hebrew is uncertain. This can be seen from the wide variety of translations:

> KJV Moreover the profit of the earth is for all: the king himself is served by the field.

NASB After all, a king who cultivates the field is an advantage to the land.

TLB And over them all is the king. Oh, for a king who is devoted to his country! Only he can bring order from this chaos.

TEV Even a king depends on the harvest.

JND Moreover the earth is every way profitable: the king (himself) is dependent on the field.

The general thought seems to be that even the highest official is dependent on the produce of the field and thus on the providence of God. All are accountable to God.

People who love money are never satisfied; they always want more (v. 10). Wealth does not buy contentment. Profits, dividends, interest payments, and capital gains whet the appetite for more. It all appears rather empty.

When a man's possessions increase, it seems that there is a corresponding increase in the number of parasites who live off his wealth, whether management consultants, tax advisers, accountants, lawyers, household employees, or sponging relatives (v. 11).

A man can wear only one suit at a time, can only eat so much in a day. So the main benefit of his wealth is to be able to look at his bank books, stocks, and bonds, and to say with other rich fools, "Soul, you have many goods laid up for many years to come; take your ease, eat, drink and be merry" (Lk 12:19).

When it comes to sound sleep, the laboring man has the advantage. Whether he has had a banquet or a snack, he can rest without care or apprehension (v. 12). Across town, the rich man is having a fitful night worrying about the market, wondering about thefts and embezzlements, and swallowing Rolaids to calm the churning sea of dyspepsia that is in his stomach.

Solomon saw that the hoarding of riches gives rise to disastrous consequences (v. 13). Here is a man who had vast reserves of wealth, but instead of using them for constructive purposes, he kept them stashed away.

All of a sudden, there was some calamity such as a market crash, and the money was all gone (v. 14). Even though the man had a son, he had nothing to leave to him. He was penniless.

Empty-handed he had come from his mother's womb, and now empty-handed he leaves this world (v. 15). In spite of all the money he had been able to accumulate during his lifetime, he dies a pauper.

Cecil Rhodes spent years exploiting the natural resources of South Africa. When he was about to die, he cried out in remorse, "I've found much in Africa. Diamonds, gold and land are mine, but now I must leave them all behind. Not a thing I've gained can be taken with me. I have not sought eternal treasures, therefore I actually have nothing at all."[1]

In verse 16, Solomon calls this "a sore evil"—a painful calamity—he could have used his money for lasting benefit. Instead of that he leaves as empty as he came, with nothing to show for all his work. He has labored for nothing.

The tragedy is compounded by the fact that the closing days of this man's life are filled with gloom, grief, worry, resentment, and sickness (v. 17). His life has been a reverse Cinderella story—from riches to rags.

Of course, there is a sense in which every man who dies leaves everything. But here the Preacher seems to point up the folly of hoarding money when it could be put to useful purposes, then losing it all, and having nothing to show for a lifetime of work.

So the best strategy is to enjoy the common activities of daily life—eating, drinking, and working (v. 18). Then no matter what happens, nothing can rob one of the pleasures he has already had. Life at best is very brief, so why not enjoy it while you can?

Solomon thought that it was ideal when God gave a man wealth and possessions and when at the same time He also gave him the ability to enjoy them, to be satisfied with his lot in life, and to enjoy his work (v. 19). This combination of circumstances was a special gift from God, or as we might say, this was "the real thing."

Such a man doesn't brood over the shortness of life or its tragedies and inequities because God keeps his mind occupied with the enjoyment of his present circumstances (v. 20).

6

A Cruel Irony

There is a cruel irony in life that lays a heavy burden on men. Solomon begins chapter 6 by discussing it.

It concerns a man to whom God has given everything that his heart could desire in the way of wealth, possessions and honor, but unfortunately God does not give him the capacity to enjoy these things (vv. 1-2). Notice that Solomon blames God for depriving him of the enjoyment of his wealth.

Then premature death robs this man of the power to enjoy his riches. He leaves it all to a stranger, not even to a son or a close relative. This certainly makes life look like an empty bubble or a malignant disease.

Even if a man has a big family and lives to a ripe, old age, these superlative mercies mean nothing if he can't enjoy life or if he doesn't have a decent burial at the end. In fact, a stillborn child is more to be envied than he (v. 3).

The untimely birth arrives as a nonperson and leaves in anonymity (v. 4). His name is covered in the obscurity of one who was never born and who never died.

Though the stillborn child never sees the sun or gets to know anything, nevertheless he enjoys rest more than the miser. He never experiences the maddening perversities of life (v. 5).

Even if the miser should live a thousand years twice over, what good is it if he has not been able to enjoy the good things of life? He shares the same fate as the stillborn child by going to the grave (v. 6).

The main reason a man works is to buy food for himself and his family (v. 7). But the odd thing is that he is never satisfied. The more his income rises, the more he wants to buy. Contentment is the carrot on the stick that forever eludes him.

So in this futile quest, the wise man doesn't have any advantage over the fool (v. 8). And even if a poor man knows how to face life better than the rest of the people, he isn't any further ahead.

It is far better to be content with the meals that are set before one than to be always craving for something additional (v. 9). This business of always lusting for more is as foolish as chasing the wind—"lustful straying about from one thing to another in quest of true satisfaction."[1]

No matter who he is, rich or poor, wise or foolish, old or young, he has already been given the name of man (v. 10). *Man* here comes from the Hebrew word *adam* and means "red clay." How can red clay dispute with the Creator?

The longer man argues, the more he multiplies futility, and he gains nothing in the process (v. 11).

The simple fact, according to Solomon (v. 12), is that no one knows what is best for him in this empty life of shadows. And no one knows what will happen on the earth after he is gone.

7

The Good and the Better

The sour note at the end of chapter 6 was that man cannot determine what is best for him under the sun. But Solomon does have ideas as to some things that are good and others that are better. That is his subject in chapter 7. In fact, the words *good* and *better* together occur here more times than in any other chapter in the Old Testament.

First, a good name is better than precious ointment. A good name, of course, signifies a good character. Precious ointment represents that which is costly and fragrant. The thought is that the most expensive perfume can never take the place of an honorable life.

Solomon says the day of death is better than the day of birth (v. 1). This is one of his statements that leaves us guessing. Did he mean this as a general axiom, or was he referring only to a man with a good name? When applied to true believers, the observation is quite true. But it is certainly not true of those who die with sins unconfessed and unforgiven.

Next Solomon decides that it is better to visit a funeral parlor than gorge oneself at a banquet (v. 2). Death is the end of all men, and when we come face to face with it, we are brought up short and forced to think about our own departure.

Every thinking person must take into account the fact of death and should have a philosophy of life which enables him to confidently face that inevitable appointment. The Gospel tells of the Saviour, who, through death, destroyed him who has the power of death, that is, the devil, and who delivers all those who, through fear of death, are subject to lifelong bondage (Heb 2:14-15).

Another "better": sorrow is better than laughter (v. 3). The Preacher was convinced that seriousness accomplishes more than levity. It sharpens the mind to grapple with the great issues of life, whereas frivolity wastes time and prevents people from coming to grips with what is important.

> I walked a mile with Pleasure;
> She chattered all the way,
> But left me none the wiser
> For all she had to say
>
> I walked a mile with Sorrow,
> And not a word said she;
> But oh, the things I learned from her
> When Sorrow walked with me!
>
> ROBERT BROWNING HAMILTON

"By the sadness of the countenance the heart is made glad" (ASV). It is one of the paradoxes of life that joy can coexist with sorrow. Even heathen philosophers have attributed a therapeutic value to suffering and sadness. But what is only moderately true for the unbeliever is more gloriously true for the child of God. Sorrows and sufferings here are the means of developing graces in his life. They give him a new appreciation of the sufferings of Christ. They enable him to comfort others who are experiencing similar trials. And they are a pledge of future glory (Ro 8:17).

The mind of a wise man maintains poise and serenity in the presence of death (v. 4). He can cope with sorrow and pressure because his roots are deep. The fool can't stand to face serious crises. He tries to drown out the sounds of life as it is with laughter and gaiety. He avoids contact with hospitals and mortuaries because his shallow resources do not equip him to stand up under the pressures of life.

There is something else that is better. "It is better to listen to the rebuke of a wise man than for one to listen to the song of fools" (v. 5). Constructive criticism instructs, corrects, and warns. The empty mirth of fools accomplishes nothing of lasting value.

The laughter of fools is like the crackling of thorns under a pot—showy and noisy but not productive (v. 6). Burning thorns may snap, crackle, and pop, but they do not make a good fuel. Little heat is generated, and the fire goes out quickly. It is noise without effectiveness, froth without body.

Even a wise man acts foolishly when he becomes a cheating oppressor (v. 7). He becomes power-mad and loses his sense of balance and restraint. And all those who indulge in bribery and graft corrupt their own minds. Once they stoop to accept payola, they lose the power to make unprejudiced judgments.

It seemed to Solomon that the end of a thing is better than the beginning (v. 8). Perhaps he was thinking of the tremendous inertia that must often be overcome to begin a project and of the drudgery and discipline that go into its early stages. Then by contrast there is the sense of achievement and satisfaction that accompanies its completion.

But it doesn't take much insight to realize that the rule does not always hold. The end of *righteous* deeds is better than the beginning, but the end of sin is worse. The latter days of Job were better than the beginning (Job 42:12), but the end of the wicked is indescribably terrible (Heb 10:31).

The Preacher was on firmer ground when he said that the patient in spirit is superior to the proud in spirit. Patience is an attractive virtue, whereas pride is the parent sin. Patience fits a man for God's approval (Ro 5:4), whereas pride fits him for destruction (Pr 16:18).

Next we are warned against the tendency to fly off the
handle (v. 9). Such lack of self-control reveals a decided
weakness of character. Someone has said that you can judge
the size of a man by the size of what it takes to make him lose
his temper. And if we nurse grudges and resentments, we
expose ourselves as fools. Intelligent people don't spoil their
lives by such nonsensical behavior.

Another foolish activity is living in the past. When we
constantly harp on the good old days and wish they would
return because they were so much better, we are living in a
world of unreality. Better to face conditions as they are and
live triumphantly in spite of them. Better to light a candle
than to curse the darkness.

Solomon's thought with regard to wisdom and an inheritance (v. 11) may be understood in several ways. First,
wisdom is good with an inheritance (KJV, NASB); it enables
the recipient to administer his bequest carefully. Second,
wisdom is good as an inheritance (JND); if one could choose
only one heritage, wisdom would be a good choice. Third,
wisdom is as good as an inheritance; it is a source of wealth.
Also it is an advantage to those who see the sun, that is, to
those who dwell on the earth. How this is so is explained in
the next verse.

Wisdom resembles money in that both afford protection
and security of sorts (v. 12). With money, one can insure
himself against physical and financial losses, whereas wisdom provides added protection from moral and spiritual
damage. That is why wisdom is superior; it preserves the
lives of its possessors, not just their material fortunes.

When we remember that Christ is the wisdom of God and
that those who find Him find life, the infinite superiority of
wisdom is obvious. In Him are hidden all the treasures of
wisdom and knowledge (Col 2:3).

One thing a wise person will do is take into account God's
sovereign control of affairs (v. 13). If He makes something
crooked, who can make it straight? In other words, who can

successfully countermand His will? His decrees are immutable and not subject to human manipulation.

In His ordering of our lives, God has seen fit to permit times of prosperity and times of adversity (v. 14). When prosperity comes, we should be glad and enjoy it. In the day of adversity, we should realize that God sends the good and the bad, happiness and trouble, so that man will not know what is going to happen next. This can be both a mercy and a frustration.

There may also be the thought that God mixes the good and the bad so that man won't be able to find fault with Him.

In either case, the conclusions are distinctly subsolar. They do not rise above flesh and blood.

We have an expression "Now I've seen everything" when we witness the unexpected, the paradoxical, the ultimate surprise. That seems to be Solomon's meaning in verse 15. In the course of his empty life, he had seen every kind of contradiction. He saw good men die young and evil men live to old age.

Since the Preacher could not detect a fixed relation between righteousness and blessing on the one hand and sin and punishment on the other, he decided that the best policy is to avoid extremes (v. 16). This shallow, unbiblical conclusion is known as the law of the golden mean.

By avoiding extreme righteousness and excessive wisdom, one might escape premature destruction. This, of course, is untrue. God's standard for His people is that they should not sin (1 Jn 2:1). And His guarantee for His people is that they are immortal till their work is done.

The other danger, in Solomon's reckoning, was extreme wickedness (v. 17). The foolhardy man can also be cut off before his time. A middle-of-the-road policy is therefore the ideal toward which we should strive, says the Preacher.

It is clear that these are man's reasonings, not God's revelations. God cannot condone sin at all. His standard is always perfection.

According to Solomon, the best policy is to take hold of this fact—the untimely fate of the overrighteous man—and not to let go of the opposite fact—the self-destruction of the profligate (v. 18). The one who fears God (by walking in the middle) will escape from both pitfalls.

This advice wrongly puts God in favor of moderation in sin and in righteousness. But it arose from Solomon's observations under the sun. Unless we remember that, we will be puzzled by such a worldly philosophy.

Solomon believes that wisdom gives more strength and protection to a man than ten rulers give to a city (v. 19), which simply means that wisdom is greater than armed might. God is not necessarily on the side of the biggest battalions.

The fact that verse 20 begins with *for* shows that it is vitally connected with what precedes. But what is the connection? The connection is that we all need the benefits of the wisdom that Solomon has been describing, because we are all imperfect. There is no one who is absolutely righteous in himself, who invariably does good and who never sins.

Generally verse 20 is taken to teach the universality of sin, and that application is legitimate. But in its context the verse "tells why we stand in need of that wisdom which has just been described" (Leupold).

A healthy sense of our own imperfection will help us to take criticisms in stride (v. 21). If we hear a servant curse us, though he is much lower on the social ladder, we can always be glad he doesn't know us better, because then he would have more to curse!

When Shimei cursed David, Abishai wanted to cut off his head, but David's reply implied that perhaps Shimei's cursing was not entirely causeless (2 Sa 16:5-14).

And we should always remember that we have been guilty of the same thing (Ec 7:22). We have cursed others in our heart many times. We can scarcely expect others to be perfect when we are so far from perfect ourselves.

That is one of the frustrations of a perfectionist. He wants everything and everyone else to be perfect, but he lives in a world of imperfection, and he himself cannot reach the goal he sets for others.

The Preacher used his extraordinary wisdom to probe into all these areas of life (v. 23). He wanted to be wise enough to solve all mysteries and unravel all the tangled skeins. But because he was making all his investigations apart from God, he found that the ultimate answers eluded him. Without special revelation, life remains an insoluble riddle.

Explanations of things as they exist are remote, inaccessible, and tremendously deep (v. 24). The world is filled with enigmas. The realm of the unknown remains unexplored. We are plagued by mysteries and unanswered questions.

In spite of his failure to come up with the answers, Solomon doggedly persevered in his search for greater wisdom and a solution to the human equation (v. 25). He wanted to understand the evil of folly and the foolishness of madness, that is, why people abandon themselves to debauchery and shame.

In that connection, he thought especially of a prostitute—a woman whose influence is more bitter than death (v. 26). Her mind is filled with subtle ways of snaring men, and those in her clutches are bound as if by chains. Anyone whose desire is to please God will escape her traps, but the man who plays around with sin is sure to cross her path and be hooked by her.

It is altogether possible that the woman here may be a type of the world or of the wisdom of the world (Col 2:8; Ja 3:15).

It seems to me that verses 27-29 express Solomon's general disappointment with his fellow human beings. When he first met anyone, he had great expectations, but after he got to know that person better, his hopes were dashed. No one met his ideal. Perhaps he would see someone who was rather attractive. He would think, *I must get to know that person better. I'd like to develop a close personal friendship.* But the more he got to know this new acquaintance, the more disillusioned he became. He found that there is no such person as the perfect stranger, and that familiarity does breed contempt.

Solomon decided to total the number of friendships in which he found a measure of real satisfaction and of fulfilled hopes. Out of all the people he had known, how many did he regard as true "soul brothers"?

He had sought repeatedly for a perfect person, but had never been able to find a single one. Everyone he met had some flaws or weaknesses of character.

All that he discovered was that good men are rare and good women rarer still. He found one man in a thousand who came close to his ideal, that is, a man who was a loyal, dependable, selfless friend.

But he couldn't find one woman in a thousand who impressed him as a reasonable approach to excellence. He did not find a woman among all those (v. 28). Such a shocking outburst of male chauvinism is incomprehensible and offensive to us today, but that is because our judgments are based on Christian principles and values. It would not be shocking to the orthodox Jew who thanks God every day that he was not born a woman. Nor would it be shocking to men of other cultures in which women are looked on as slaves or mere property.

Commentators go through interpretative gymnastics to soften the force of Solomon's harsh words here, but their well-intentioned efforts are misdirected. The fact is that the Preacher probably meant exactly what he said. And his conclusion is still shared by men throughout the world whose outlook is earthbound and carnal.

Solomon's view of women was terribly one-sided. G. Campbell Morgan gave a more balanced view when he wrote:

> The influence of women is most powerful for good or for ill. I once heard one of the keenest of observers say that no great

movement for the uplifting of humanity has been generated in
human history but that woman's influence had much to do
with it. Whether so superlative a statement is capable of
substantiation I do not know; but I believe there is a great
element of truth in it. It is equally true that the part that
women have taken in corrupting the race has been terrible.
When the womanhood of a nation is noble, the national life is
held in strength. When it is corrupt, the nation is doomed.
Woman is the last stronghold of good or of evil. Compassion
and cruelty are superlative in her.[1]

Solomon later redeemed himself by writing one of
literature's noblest tributes to womanhood—Proverbs 31. In
Ecclesiastes he writes from the earthly plane of human prej-
udice, but in Proverbs 31 he writes from the lofty peak of
divine revelation.

With the advent of the Christian faith, woman has reached
the summit in her rise to dignity and respect. The Lord Jesus
is her truest Friend and Emancipator.

As Solomon pondered his unending disappointment in the
people he had met, he correctly concluded that man has
fallen from his original condition (v. 29). How true! God
made man in His own image and after His likeness. But man
sought out many sinful schemes which marred and distorted
the divine image in him.

Even in his fallen condition, man still has an intuitive
hunger to find perfection. He goes through life looking for
the perfect partner, the perfect job, the perfect everything.
But he cannot find perfection in others or in himself. The
trouble is that his search is confined to the sphere *under the
sun.* Only one perfect life has ever been lived on this earth,
that is the life of the Lord Jesus Christ. But now He is above
the sun, exalted at the right hand of God. And God satisfies
man's hunger for perfection with Christ—no one else, no
other thing.

8

The Wisdom of Wisdom

In spite of the failure of human wisdom to solve all his problems, Solomon still admired the wise man above others (8:1). No one else is as qualified to search out the hidden meaning of things. As far as the Preacher-King was concerned, wisdom is even mirrored in one's physical appearance. His face is radiant, and an otherwise stern visage is softened.

Wisdom teaches one how to act in the presence of the king, whether that king be conceived as God or as an earthly monarch. It inculcates obedience first of all. The Hebrew of the latter part of this verse is obscure, as is seen by the following translations:

> and that in regard of the oath of God (KJV).
> because of the oath before God (NASB).

The oath here may refer to one's pledge of allegiance to the government or to God's oath by which He authorized kings to rule (e.g., see Ps 89:35).

The obscurity continues in verse 3. We may understand this verse to advise leaving the king's presence without delay when unpleasantness develops. Or it may advise against making a hasty exit, either in anger, disobedience, insolence, or in quitting one's job (KJV, NASB).

Certainly the thrust of the passage is that it is unwise to cross a king, since he has wide authority to do as he pleases.

Whenever a king speaks, his word is backed with power (v. 4). It is supreme and is not subject to challenge by his subjects.

Those who obey the king's commandment need not fear the royal displeasure (v. 5). Wisdom teaches a person what is appropriate, both as to time and procedure in obeying the royal edicts.

There's a right and wrong way of doing things, and a right and wrong time as well (v. 6). The trouble that lies heavy upon man is that he cannot always discern these moments of destiny.

There is so much that he cannot know or do. He cannot know the future—what is going to happen or how it will happen (v. 7).

He cannot prevent his spirit from departing or determine the exact time of his death (v. 8). He cannot obtain discharge from war—especially the war that death is relentlessly waging against him. He cannot win a reprieve by any form of wickedness that he may give himself over to.

These are some of the things that Solomon observed when he studied life under the sun, in a world where one man crushes another under his heel, "wherein a man has exercised authority over another man to his hurt" (v. 9).

So much of life is shallow (v. 10). The crook dies and is buried. He once made trips to the place of worship. Now that he is gone, people praise him for his piety in the very city where he used to carry on his crooked schemes. Religion can be a facade to cover up dishonesty. It is all so empty and meaningless.

Endless delays in the trial and punishment of criminals only serve to encourage lawlessness and create contempt for the judicial system (v. 11). While it is important to guarantee that every defendant has a fair trial, it is possible to overprotect the criminal at the expense of his victim. Fair, impartial justice meted out promptly serves as a deterrent to crime. On the other hand, interminable postponements make offenders more fixed in their determination to break the law. They reason that they can get away with it or at least get a light sentence.

Although Solomon had seen some cases that seemed to be exceptions, he believed that those who fear God will fare best in the long run (v. 12). Even if a habitual criminal lives to an old age, that exception doesn't invalidate the fact that righteousness is rewarded eventually and that the way of the transgressor is hard.

The Preacher was confident that the wicked person is an ultimate loser (v. 13). By his failure to fear God, he dooms himself to a short life. His life is transient as a shadow (KJV).

Solomon seems to alternate between general rules and glaring exceptions (v. 14). Sometimes an upright man seems to be punished as if he were a transgressor. And sometimes a lawbreaker seems to be rewarded as if he were a decent, honest citizen. These violations of what ought to be caused the Philosopher-King to be disgusted with the emptiness of life.

The only logical policy, as far as he was concerned, was to enjoy life while you can (v. 15). There is nothing better than to eat, drink, and have a good time. This will stand by a person as he toils on throughout the life that God gives him in this world. No pie-in-the-sky philosophy for Solomon. He wanted his pie here and now.

So Solomon devoted himself to finding all the answers (v. 16). He trained his mind in the study of philosophy, determined to get to the bottom of the activities of life—a task in which one gets no sleep day or night.

Then he found that God has so arranged things that man cannot put all the parts of the puzzle together (v. 17). No matter how hard he tries, he will fail. And no matter how wise he is, he won't find answers to all the questions.

9

Live It Up Before You Die

In chapter 9, the Preacher pondered all these things, taking in as wide and exhaustive a view as possible. He saw that good people and wise people and all that they do are in the hands of God (v. 1). But whether what will happen to them is a sign of God's love or hatred, no one knows. The entire future is unknown and unknowable, and anything can happen.

Ecclesiastes didn't know whether God acted in love or hate but we know (Ro 8:28; Heb 12:6).

What makes it all so enigmatical is that the righteous and the wicked, the good and the evil, the clean and the unclean, the worshiper and the nonworshiper all end in the same place—the grave (v. 2). As far as escaping death is concerned, the good man has no advantage over the wicked. Those who put themselves under oaths are in the same predicament as those who shun an oath.

This is the great calamity of life—that death eventually claims all classes of men (v. 3). People can live outrageous, insane lives, and after that—death. What is this but gross injustice if death is the end of existence?

As long as man is alive, there is hope; that is, he has something to look forward to (v. 4). In that sense, a living dog is better off than a dead lion. Here the dog is spoken of, not as man's best friend, but as one of the lowest, meanest forms of animal life. The lion is the king of beasts, powerful and magnificent.

The living at least know that they will die, but the dead don't know anything about what's going on in the world (v. 5).

This verse is constantly used by false teachers to prove that the soul sleeps in death, that consciousness ceases when the last breath is taken. But it is senseless to build a doctrine of the hereafter on this verse, or on this book, for that matter. As has been repeatedly emphasized, Ecclesiastes represents man's best conclusions as he searches for answers "under the sun." It sets forth deductions based on observations and on logic but not on divine revelation. It is what a wise man might think if he did not have a Bible.

What would you think if you saw a person die and watched his body be lowered into the grave, knowing that it would eventually return to dust? You might think, *That's the end. My friend knows nothing now; he can't enjoy any activities that are going on; he has forgotten and will soon be forgotten.*

And so it is, thought Solomon. Once a person has died, there is no more love, hatred, jealousy, or any other human emotion (v. 6). Never again will he participate in any of this world's activities and experiences.

So once again the Preacher comes back to his basic conclusion—live your life, have a good time, enjoy your food, cheer your heart with wine (v. 7). God has already approved what you do, or, better, it's all right with God.

Wear bright clothing, not mourning attire (v. 8). And put perfume on your head rather than ashes. Some think the world should be for fun and frolic, and so did Solomon.

The joys of the marriage relationship should also be exploited to the full as long as possible (v. 9). It's a vain, empty life anyway, so the best thing is to make the most of it. Enjoy every day because that's all you are going to get out of your toil and trouble.

Verses 7-9 are strikingly similar to a passage in the Gilgamesh epic, an ancient Babylonian account of creation.

> Since the gods created man
> Death they ordained for man,
> Life in their hands they hold,
> Thou, O Gilgamesh, fill indeed thy belly.
> Day and night be thou joyful,
> Daily ordain gladness,
> Day and night rage and be merry,
> Let thy garments be bright,
> Thy head purify, wash with water.
> Desire thy children which thy hand possesses.
> A wife enjoy in thy bosom.[1]

The significance of this is not that one was copied from the other, but that man's wisdom under the sun leads to the same conclusion. I was impressed with this fact when I read Denis Alexander's summary of what humanism offers us today.

> The humanist model does seem a very big pill to swallow. As a representative of a late twentieth-century generation of under-thirties, I am first asked to believe that I am the result of a purely random evolutionary process. The only prerequisites for this process are the presence of matter, time and chance. Because by some strange whim of fate, I and other men are the only physical structures which happen to have been bestowed with a consciousness of their own existence, I am supposed to think of both myself and others as being in some way more valuable than other physical structures such as rabbits, trees or stones, even though in a hundred years time the atoms of my decayed body may well be indistinguishable from theirs. Furthermore the mass of vibrating atoms in my head are supposed to have more ultimate meaning than those in the head of a rabbit.
>
> At the same time I am told that death is the end of the line. In the time-scale of evolution my life is a vapour which soon vanishes. Whatever feelings of justice or injustice I may have

in this life, all my strivings, all my greatest decisions, will be ultimately swallowed up in the on-going march of time. In a few million years' time, a mere drop compared with the total history of the earth. The memory of the greatest literature, the greatest art, the greatest lives will be buried in the inexorable decay of the Second Law of Thermodynamics. Hitler and Martin Luther King, James Sewell and Francis of Assisi, Chairman Mao and Robert Kennedy, all will be obliterated in the unthinking void.

So, I am told, I must make the best of a bad job. Even though I have strong feelings of transcendence, a deep sense that I am more than just a blind whim of evolution, I must nevertheless forget such troubling questions, and concern myself with the real problems of trying to live responsibly in society. Even though my job involves studying man's brain as a machine, like any other of nature's machines, I must still believe that man has some special intrinsic worth which is greater than an animal's worth, and while my emotions tell me that it may be true, I am not given any more objective reason for believing it.[2]

The maxim in verse 10, one of the best known in the book, is often used by believers to encourage zeal and diligence in Christian service, and the advice is sound. But in its context, it really means to seize every possible pleasure and enjoyment while you can, because you won't be able to work, invent, think, or know anything in the grave, to which you are irreversibly heading.

As someone has said, the advice given in this verse is excellent, but the reason is utterly bad. And even the advice must be restricted to activities that are legitimate, helpful, and edifying in themselves.

Another thing that Solomon observed is that luck and chance play a big part in life (v. 11). The race isn't always won by the fastest runner. The bravest soldiers don't always win the war. The wisest don't always enjoy the best meals. The cleverest are not always the richest. And the most capable do not always rise to the presidency. Bad luck dogs everyone's steps. Time and chance are factors that play an important role in success and failure. When the billionaire J. Paul Getty was asked to explain his success, he replied, "Some people find oil. Others don't."

And no one knows when bad luck will strike (v. 12). Like fishes in a net or birds in a trap, man is overtaken by bad fortune or even by death. He never knows which bullet has his name on it.

Still another heartache in life is that wisdom is not always appreciated (vv. 13-15). To illustrate this, there was a small city with few inhabitants and therefore poorly defended. A powerful king surrounded it with artillery and prepared to break through the walls.

When the situation seemed hopeless, a man who was poor but very wise came forward with a plan that saved the city. At the moment he was a hero, but then he was quickly forgotten.

It grieved the Preacher that though wisdom is superior to power, yet the advice of the poor man was subsequently scorned (v. 16). As soon as the crisis was past, no one was interested in what he had to say.

This parable has a definite evangelistic ring to it. The city is like man's soul—small and defenseless. The great king is Satan, bent on invasion and destruction (2 Co 4:4; Eph 2:2). The deliverer is the Saviour—poor (2 Co 8:9) and wise (1 Co 1:24; Col 2:3). Though He provided deliverance, yet how little He is honored and appreciated! Most people of the world live as if He had never died. And even Christians are often careless about remembering Him in His appointed way, that is, in the Lord's Supper.

Yet in spite of man's ingratitude and indifference it is still true that the words of wise men spoken quietly are worth more than the shouting tirades of a powerful ruler among fools (v. 17).

Wisdom is superior to armaments and munitions (v. 18). In

2 Samuel 20:14-22 we read how a wise woman delivered the city of Abel of Beth-maachah when Joab besieged it.

But one sinful dolt can undo a lot of good that the wise person accomplishes, just as little foxes can spoil the vines.

10

Portrait of a Wise Man and a Fool

When flies get caught in perfume or ointment and die, they cause it to give off a terrible stench (10:1). And in this, there is an analogy to human behavior. A man may build up a reputation for wisdom and honor, yet he can ruin it all by a single misstep. People will remember one little indiscretion and forget years of worthy achievements. Any person can ruin his reputation by speaking just three words of the wrong kind in public.

The right hand is generally more dexterous, the left more awkward. The wise man knows the right way to do a thing; the fool is an awkward bungler (v. 2).

Even when a fool does something simple, like walking along the street, he betrays a lack of common sense (v. 3). He says to everyone that he is a fool, which may mean that he calls every one else stupid or that he shows his own ignorance in all he does. The latter is probably the thought.

If a ruler explodes in anger at you, it is best not to quit in a huff (v. 4). It is better to be meek and submissive. This will be more apt to pacify him and atone for serious mistakes.

Another inconsistency which bothered Solomon in this mixed-up world proceeded from unwise decisions and injustices by rulers (v. 5). Often men are appointed to positions without suitable qualifications, while capable men waste their talents on menial tasks (v. 6). Thus slaves often ride on horses, while princes have to travel by foot (v. 7). Such inequities exist in politics, in industry, in the military services and in religious life as well. Those who dig ditches to harm others will be victims of their own malice (v. 8). Chickens have a way of coming home to roost.

Whoever breaks down a wall of stones, either for unlawful entry, or mischief, or to change a property line can expect to be bitten by a serpent or to pay for it in some other unpleasant way.

Even legitimate activities have risks attached (v. 9). The quarryman is in danger of being injured by stones, and the log-splitter is endangered by the ax.

It's a good idea to work with sharp tools (v. 10). Otherwise it takes a lot more labor to get the job done. The time spent sharpening the ax is more than compensated by the time and effort saved. Wisdom teaches shortcuts and labor-saving devices. "Wisdom prepares the way for success" (Leupold).

What good is a charmer if the snake bites before the charm begins? (v. 11). Or as we might say, why lock the barn after the horse is stolen? Things must often be done on time in order to be valuable and effective.

The words of a wise man bring him favor because they are gracious (v. 12). The words of a fool prove to be his downfall.

He may begin with harmless nonsense, but by the time he is through, he is engaging in malicious madness (v. 13).

A fool doesn't know when to stop (v. 14). Words, words, words. He talks on and on as if he knew everything, but he doesn't. His endless chatter almost inevitably includes boasts of what he will do in the future. He is like the rich fool who said, "This is what I will do: I will tear down my barns, and build larger ones; and there I will store all my grain and my goods. 'And I will say to my soul, "Soul, you have many goods laid up for many years to come; take your ease, eat, drink, and be merry' ' ' '' (Lk 12:18-19). But he does not know what is going to happen next. He would be better advised to say, "If the Lord will, we shall live, and also do this, or that" (Ja 4:15, KJV).

He exhausts himself by his inefficient and unproductive work (v. 15). He can't even see the obvious or find the way to anything as conspicuous as a city. Perhaps we could add that he doesn't know enough to come in out of the rain. His ignorance in such simple matters makes his plans for the future all the more ludicrous.

Pity the country whose ruler is immature and impressionable like a child and whose legislators carouse in the morning instead of attending to their duties (v. 16).

The fortunate country is one in which the king is a man of character and nobility, and in which the other leaders manifest propriety and self-control by eating for strength and not for dissipation (v. 17).

Continued laziness and neglect cause a house to fall apart, whether that house represents a government or an individual life (v. 18). Any roof will leak unless the owner provides regular maintenance.

Meal time is a happy time (v. 19). Wine adds sparkle to life. Money answers everything.

Did Solomon really believe that money is the key to all pleasure? Perhaps he simply meant that money can buy whatever man needs in the way of foods and drinks. Or maybe he was just quoting the drunken rulers of verse 16 when they were warned where their excesses would lead (v. 18). The fact, as someone has said, is that money is the universal passport to everywhere except heaven and the universal provider of everything except happiness. A man's life does not consist in the abundance of the things he possesses.

Be careful not to speak evil against the king or his wealthy subordinates (v. 20). You may think that nobody hears. But even the walls have ears, and some unsuspected bird will carry the message to the royal palace. "Indiscretions have a way of sprouting wings."

11

Spread the Good Around

In verse 1 of chapter 11, bread is used symbolically for the grain from which it is made. To cast bread upon the water may refer to the practice of sowing in flooded areas, or it may mean carrying on grain trade by sea. In any case, the thought is that a widespread and wholesale distribution of what is good will result in a generous return in the time of harvest.

This verse is true of the Gospel. We may not see immediate results as we share the bread of life, but the eventual harvest is sure.

Giving a portion to seven, even to eight suggests two things—unrestrained generosity or diversification of business enterprises (v. 2). If the first is meant, the idea is that we should show uncalculating kindness while we can, because a time of calamity and misfortune may come when this will not be possible. Most people save for a rainy day; this verse counsels to adopt a spirit of unrestricted liberality because of the uncertainties of life.

Or the thought may be, Don't put all your eggs in one basket. Invest in several interests so that if one fails, you will still be able to carry on with the others. This is known as diversification.

Verse 3 carries on the thought of the previous one, especially with regard to the unknown evil which may happen on earth. It suggests that there is a certain inevitability and finality about the calamities of life. Just as surely as rain-laden clouds empty themselves on the earth, so surely do troubles and trials come to the sons of men. And once a tree is overthrown, it remains a fallen monarch. Its destiny is sealed.

A wider application of the verse is given in the poem:

> As a tree falls, so must it lie,
> As a man lives, so must he die,
> As a man dies, so must he be,
> All through the years of eternity.
>
> JOHN RAY

It is possible to be too cautious (v. 14). If you wait till conditions are perfect, you will accomplish nothing. There are usually some wind and some clouds. If you wait for zero wind conditions, you will never get the seed into the fields. If you wait until there is no risk of rain, the crops will rot before they are harvested. "The man who waits for certainty will wait forever."

Since we don't know everything, we have to muddle along with what knowledge we do have (v. 5). We don't understand the movements of the wind (NASB), how the spirit comes to a fetus (TLB), or how the bones are formed in the womb of a pregnant woman (KJV). Neither do we understand all that God does or why He does it.

Since we don't know this, the best policy is to fill the day with all kinds of productive work (v. 6). We have no way of knowing which activities will succeed. Maybe they all will.

In spreading the Word of God, success is guaranteed. But it is still true that some methods are more fruitful than others. So we should be untiring, versatile, ingenious, and faithful in Christian service.

Then too we should sow in the morning of life and not slack off in the evening. We are called to unremitting service.

The light, in verse 7, may refer to the bright and shining days of youth. It's great to be young—to be healthy, strong, and vivacious. But no matter how many years of vigor and prosperity a man enjoys, he should be aware that days of darkness are almost sure to come (v. 8). The aches and pains of old age are inevitable. It's a dreary, empty time of life.

It is hard to know whether verse 9 is sincere advice or the cynicism of a disillusioned old man. In either case, the idea is to enjoy youth while you can. Do what your heart desires and see as much as you can. But just remember that eventually God will bring you into judgment, that is, the judgment of old age, which seemed to Solomon like divine retribution for the sins of early life.

12

The Decline and Fall of the Human Body

Nowhere in literature is there a more classic description of old age than in the verses of chapter 12. They are enough to make the editor of the *Journal of Gerontology* eat his heart out. The meaning does not lie on the surface because it is presented as an allegory. But soon the picture emerges of a doddering old man, a walking geriatric museum, shuffling his way irresistibly to the grave.

The doleful picture of age and senility is a warning to young people to remember their Creator in the days of their youth (v. 1). Notice Solomon does not say their Lord or Saviour or Redeemer but their Creator. That is the only way Solomon could know God from his vantage point under the sun. But even at that, the advice is good. Young people *should* remember their Creator before the sunset time of life, when the days are evil and cruel and the years are totally lacking in pleasure and enjoyment. The aspiration of every young person should be that which is expressed in the following lines by Thomas H. Gill.

> Lord, in the fullness of my might,
> I would for Thee be strong;
> While runneth o'er each dear delight,
> To Thee should soar my song.

> I would not give the world my heart,
>   And then profess Thy love;
> I would not feel my strength depart,
>   And then Thy service prove.
>
> I would not with swift winged zeal
>   On the world's errands go:
> And labour up the heav'nly hill
>   With weary feet and slow.
>
> O not for Thee my weak desires,
>   My poorer baser part!
> O not for Thee my fading fires,
>   The ashes of my heart.
>
> O choose me in my golden time,
>   In my dear joys have part!
> For Thee the glory of my prime
>   The fullness of my heart.[1]

Old age is the time when the lights grow dim, both physically and emotionally (v. 2). The days are dreary, and the nights are long. Gloom and depression settle in.

The clouds return after the rain. Even in earlier years, there was a certain amount of rain, that is, of trouble and discouragement. But then the sun would emerge and the spirit would quickly bounce back. Now it seems that the sunny days are gone, and after each spell of rain, the clouds appear with the promise of more.

Now the body of the old man is presented under the figure of a house (v. 3). The keepers of the house are the arms and hands, once strong and active, now wrinkled, gnarled, and trembling with Parkinson's disease.

The strong men are the legs and thighs, no longer straight and athletic, but bowed like parenthesis marks, as if buckling under the weight of the body.

"The grinders cease because they are few" (KJV), that is, the teeth are no longer able to chew because there are too few uppers to meet the remaining lowers. The dentist would say there is inadequate occlusion.

Those that look through the windows are dimmed. The eyes have been failing steadily. First they needed bifocals, then trifocals, then surgery for cataracts. Now they can only read extra large type with the use of a magnifying glass.

The doors on the street are shut. This refers, of course, to the ears. Everything has to be repeated over and over. Loud noises, like the grinding of the mill, are very low and indistinct.

The old man suffers from insomnia; he is up bright and early, when the birds first begin to chirp or the rooster crows.

All the daughters of song are brought low; the vocal chords are seriously impaired. The voice is crackling and unsteady, and song is out of the question.

They develop acrophobia, that is, they now have a great fear of heights, whether ladders, views from tall buildings or plane rides (v. 5).

And terrors are in the way. They have lost self-confidence, are afraid to go out alone, or to go out at night.

The blossoming almond tree is generally taken to picture the white hair, first in rich profusion, then falling to the ground.

The grasshopper may be interpreted in two ways. First, the grasshopper shall be a burden (KJV), that is, even the lightest objects are too heavy for the old person to carry. Or, the grasshopper dragging itself along (NASB), caricatures the old man, bent over and twisted, inching forward in jerky, erratic movements.

Desire fails in the sense that natural appetites diminish or cease altogether. Food no longer has flavor or zest, and other basic drives peter out. Sexual vigor is gone. The caperberry (NASB) was supposed to be aphrodisiac, stimulating sexual desire.

This degenerative process takes place because man is going to the long-lasting home of death and the grave, and soon his funeral procession will be moving down the street.

And so the advice of the wise man is to remember the

Creator before the silver cord is snapped, or the golden bowl is broken, or the pitcher is broken at the fountain, or the wheel is broken at the cistern (v. 6). It is difficult to assign precise meanings to all of these figures.

The snapping of the silver chord probably refers to the breaking of the tender thread of life when the spirit is released from the body. The blind poet, Fanny Crosby, apparently understood it in this way when she wrote,

> Some day the silver chord will break
> And I no more as now shall sing
> But oh the joy when I shall wake
> Within the palace of the King.[2]

The golden bowl has been understood to mean the cranial cavity, and its breaking to be a poetic picture of the cessation of the mind at the time of death.

The broken pitcher and wheel taken together could be a reference to the circulatory system with the breakdown of systolic and diastolic blood pressure.

Rigor mortis sets in, and the body begins its return to dust, while the spirit returns to God who gave it (v. 7). Or so it seemed to Solomon. In the case of a believer, his conclusion is true. But in the case of an unbeliever, the spirit goes to hades, there to await the Great White Throne Judgment. Then the spirit will be reunited with the body and the entire person cast into the lake of fire (Rev 20:12-14).

And so Solomon comes full-circle to where he began —with the basic tenet that life under the sun is vanity, meaningless, futile, and empty (v. 8). His pathetic refrain reminds us of the little girl who went to the fair and stayed too long.

> I wanted the music to play on forever—
>   Have I stayed too long at the fair?
> I wanted the clown to be constantly clever—
>   Have I stayed too long at the fair?
> I bought me blue ribbons to tie up my hair,
>   But I couldn't find anybody to care

The merry-go-round is beginning to slow now,
Have I stayed too long at the fair?

I wanted to live in a carnival city, with
laughter and love everywhere.
I wanted my friends to be thrilling and witty.
I wanted somebody to care.
I found my blue ribbons all shiny and new,
But now I've discovered them no longer blue.
The merry-go-round is beginning to taunt me—
Have I stayed too long at the fair?
There is nothing to win and no one to want me—
Have I stayed too long at the fair?[3]

BILLY BARNES

As we come here to Solomon's last reference to the emptiness of life under the sun, I am reminded of a story which E. Stanley Jones used to tell. On board ship he saw a very corpulent couple, their faces bovine, who lived from meal to meal. They were retired on plenty—and nothing.

They were angry with the table stewards for not giving them super-service. They seemed to be afraid they might starve between courses. Their physical appetites seemed the one thing that mattered to them. I never saw them reading a book or paper. They sat between meals and stared out, apparently waiting for the next meal. One night I saw them sitting thus and staring blankly, when a bright idea flashed across the dull brain of the man. He went to the mantelpiece and picked up the vases, and looked into them, and then returned to his wife with the news: "They're empty!" I came very near laughing. He was right; "They're empty!" But it wasn't merely the vases! The souls and brains of both of them were empty. They had much in their purses, but nothing in their persons; and that was their punishment. They had security with boredom—no adventure. They had expanding girths and narrowing horizons.[4]

Besides being wise himself, the Preacher shared his knowledge with others (v. 9). He sought to transmit his wisdom in the form of proverbs, after carefully weighing them and testing them for accuracy.

He chose his words carefully, trying to combine what was comforting, pleasant, and true (v. 10). It was like preparing a nutritious meal, then serving it with a sprig of parsley.

The teachings of wise men are like sharp, pointed instruments, plain, direct, and convincing (v. 11). And the collected sayings from the one Shepherd are like well-driven nails or pins that give stability to a tent. They provide strength and are also pegs on which we may hang our thoughts.

Most Bible versions capitalize the word Shepherd, indicating that the translators understood it as referring to God. However, it should also be remembered that in Eastern thought, a king is looked on as a shepherd. Homer said, "All kings are shepherds of the people." So it could be that King Solomon was referring to himself as the one shepherd. This interpretation fits into the context more smoothly.

There is no thought that Solomon had exhausted the subject (v. 12). He could have written more, but he warns his readers that the conclusion would be the same. There is no end to the writing and publishing of books, and it would be exhausting to read them all. But why bother, because all they could reveal would be the vanity of life.

His final conclusion may give the impression that he has at last risen above the sun (v. 13). He says to fear God and keep His commandments, because this is the whole duty of man. But we must keep in mind that the fear of God here is not the same as saving faith. It is the slavish terror of a creature before his Creator. And the commandments do not necessarily mean the law of God as revealed in the Old Testament. Rather they might mean any commands which God has instinctively written on the hearts of mankind.

In other words, we need not assign a high degree of spiritual insight to Solomon's words. They may be nothing more than what a wise person would conclude from natural intuition and from practical experience.

This is the whole of man—not just the whole duty but the basic elements that make for a full and happy life.

The motive for fearing and obeying God here is the certainty of coming judgment (v. 14). We can be eternally grateful as believers that the Saviour has delivered us from this kind of fear.

"There is no fear in love, but perfect love casts out fear, because fear involves punishment, and the one who fears is not perfected in love" (1 Jn 4:18).

We do not trust and obey because of fear but because of love. Through His finished work on Calvary, we have the assurance that we will never come into judgment but have passed from death into life (Jn 5:24). Now we can say:

> There is no condemnation,
> There is no hell for me,
> The torment and the fire
> My eyes shall never see;
> For me there is no sentence,
> For me there is no sting
> Because the Lord who loves me
> Shall shield me with His wing.
>
> PAUL GERHARDT

How to Find What Solomon Sought!

In his search, Solomon never found satisfaction. The book of Ecclesiastes contains no suggestion that he was satisfied with anything he tried. In fact, the word ''satisfaction'' never occurs in the book.

We have already suggested the reason for his failure. He was searching under the sun, and nothing under the sun can fully and finally fill the heart of man.

What it boils down to is that a person has to get above the sun! But that is a vague, mystical, intangible sort of statement. Why do we have to get above the sun, and how do we do it?

As for the ''why,'' the answer is this. God has so created us that we can only experience lasting peace and pleasure through coming to know Him in a personal and intimate way. We were made to love the Lord and enjoy Him forever, and we can never find fulfillment short of that destiny.

But then how can we know God in this way? That is the crucial question.

When God created man, the lines of communication were open and clear. Man walked in fellowship with his Creator. But then a snag developed! Adam sinned. This changed the entire picture. Fellowship was broken. Diplomatic relations were severed. Man became a rebel against his Maker.

Since then distance and hostility have separated the creature and his Creator. Adam passed down a legacy of rebellion and sin to all his descendants. Man by nature has been separated from God.

God, for His part, has never ceased to love man. But because He is holy, He cannot wink at sin or disregard it. His righteousness demands that the penalty of sin be paid, and that penalty is eternal death. If we have to pay the penalty of our own sins, then we are doomed eternally. Nothing we could do would ever atone for our sins. Left to ourselves we are helpless and hopeless, and candidates for hell.

To save us from endless punishment, God sent His Son to die as our Substitute. That is what Calvary is all about. On the Cross the Lord Jesus Christ suffered as our Representative. He paid the penalty that our sins deserved. He died the death that we should have died. As the sinless One, He bled and died in behalf of sinners.

To show that He was well-pleased with the work of His Son, God raised Him from the dead and exalted Him to His own right hand in heaven.

So that brings us to our question—how can we know God in a personal way? Jesus answered the question in the words of John 14:6: "I am the way, and the truth, and the life; no one comes to the Father but through Me." Which simply means that we must avail ourselves of His work on the Cross if we are ever to be reconciled to God.

In order to do this we must first repent. This calls for an about-face with regard to sin. It involves an honest acknowledgment of the fact that we are sinners. We must take sides with God against ourselves, confessing that we are guilty, lost, helpless, hopeless, and worthy of eternal punishment. But repentance is not enough.

We must also realize that the Lord Jesus died to save us from sin. Here it is not sufficient to assent to the fact that He died in a general way for all mankind. It must be intensely personal—I must believe that He died for *me*.

And that brings us to the decisive step. By a definite act of faith, I must receive Jesus Christ as my Lord and Saviour. I must commit myself to Him in utter confidence that He will remove my sins with all their guilt, and make me fit for God's heaven. From my heart I must say something like this:

> O God, I am a sinner. I richly deserve to go to hell. But I believe that the Lord Jesus died as my sin-bearer. He endured the punishment that I should have endured for all eternity. And so I accept Him. Renouncing any other hope of salvation, I receive Him as my Saviour, and determine to acknowledge Him henceforth as the Lord of my life.

Whenever a person thus receives the Lord Jesus Christ by faith, he is born again, saved, converted. He receives immunity from judgment and the guarantee of eternal life. Hostilities come to an end, and a state of peace with God begins.

Now life has meaning. A person finds the reason for his existence. Every deepest longing of the heart finds its answer in Christ. Jesus is the Fountainhead of all true pleasure. He alone gives purpose to living, and a bright hope to dying. The man who finds Christ can say at last, "For He has satisfied the thirsty soul, and the hungry soul He has filled with what is good" (Ps 107:9).

Of course salvation is just the beginning. After birth comes growth. And the Christian life is a matter of growing in grace and in the knowledge of the Lord Jesus. It does not necessarily get easier but it does get better. It is like the light of day that begins at dawn and grows to the brilliance of the splendor of noonday. It is a charmed life, a growing surprise, an increasing enjoyment.

Stanley Jones was right when he said that the man who accepts Christ hugs himself ever afterward that he had sense enough to do it. Jesus really satisfies.

APPENDIX B

My Own Ecclesiastes

Although I cannot lay claim to the many achievements of which Solomon boasted, I can say this—I have found fulfillment in life. I view my life not as a hopeless end, but as an endless hope. It has been characterized not by vanity, but by reality. Life has not been a striving after wind but the continuous enjoyment of the living God.

I have had a good life. "The lines have fallen to me in pleasant places; indeed, my heritage is beautiful to me" (Ps 16:6). With thankfulness I confess that goodness and mercy have followed me all the days of my life, and my cup overflows (Ps 23:5-6).

I am a satisfied man, that is, I have found perfect and complete satisfaction in the Lord Jesus Christ. He has satisfied my thirsty soul, and filled my hungry heart with good things (Ps 107:9). Don't misunderstand me—I am not satisfied with what I am in myself. My spiritual attainments have been disappointing, and my service for the Lord unprofitable. But I can find no fault in Him. All that this heart of mine can desire is found in Him.

I have become fabulously wealthy. First of all, I am a child of God, an heir of God and a joint heir with Jesus Christ. All things are mine, and I am Christ's and Christ is God's (1 Co 3:22-23). That is the true wealth that brings contentment. But even in another sense I have been wealthy—not in the abundance of my possessions but in the fewness of my wants. Like Hudson Taylor, I have enjoyed the luxury of having few things to care for. I have aspired to be like the Man of Galilee—the perfect Man "who owned nothing and left nothing but the clothes that he wore" (Denney). And this freedom from covetousness has brought me the contentment that money cannot buy.

I can never thank God enough for all His providential dealings in my life. I thank Him for the gift of physical life. More than once in my childhood He miraculously preserved me from death. Once I was so low, my mother turned away from the bed so she would not see the final death struggle.

Then too I thank Him for the gift of physical sight. According to all the laws of medical science, I ought to be blind. But God in great mercy did the impossible, and I have probably been able to read more books in my lifetime than the average person with normal vision.

But most of all I thank the Lord for the gift of eternal life. It was all so undeserved—that God should send His lovely Son to die as my sin-bearing Substitute, and that He should give me pardon and forgiveness through faith in Him. It is more than I will ever be able to understand.

I praise God for His keeping power, for the way He has preserved me from falling. When I think of my own weakness, of my proneness to wander, and of the appalling power of temptation, both from within and without, I marvel at His goodness in holding me up.

I shall always be grateful for the privilege of serving such a Master. I have not found Him a severe Person, taking up what He did not lay down, and reaping what He did not sow (Lk 19:21). Instead I have found Him to be compassionate, patient, forgiving, and generous. Like the Hebrew slave, I can truthfully say, "I love my master; I will not go out free" (Ex 21:5).

I think of the marvelous answers to prayer which I have experienced. It is so wonderful that the great God should hear my prayers and answer them in ways which, according to the laws of chance or probability, could never happen.

And I cannot forget the treasure I have found in the sacred Scriptures. No Klondike prospector was ever more thrilled with his nuggets of gold than I have been with new gems of Bible truth.

Then too I think with unceasing gratitude of how the Lord has enriched my life through the fellowship and friendship of His family. He raised this poor man from the dust, lifted him from the ash heap, and made him sit with the princes of His people (Ps 113:7). I can say with an old saint, "My intercourse has been with the excellent of the earth." What a benediction God's people have been to me!

Does this mean that there have been no sorrows in my life? Of course not. I have had my share. But not one has been random or accidental. All have been purposeful, educative, and disciplinary.

Sickness and disabilities have come as well. Like Paul I have prayed three times for the removal of a thorn in the flesh, but the thorn was not removed. At other times I have prayed for the restoration of something I thought I couldn't live a normal life without, but it wasn't restored. But it would be a sin to complain. I always came to realize that His grace is sufficient and His way is best. If I could have chosen the ingredients of my life, including sorrow, sickness and impairments, I wouldn't want it any other way than the way He has planned.

I have not been immune to criticism or even betrayal. Much of the criticism was justified; the rest was sanctified to His glory, to my good, and hopefully to the blessing of others. Even betrayal enabled me to share the fellowship of His sufferings in a way that otherwise could not be.

Far greater than all the minuses have been the pluses. I often think of the privilege of traveling for the Lord throughout North America, Europe, and Asia. Wherever I went, I met the forever-family-of-Jesus. These were people I had never known before, yet immediately our hearts were knit together in love. They received me as an angel of God, and the companionship of love will never end.

Though I have had no home or family of my own, I have proved the reality of His promise—I have received a hundredfold more in this time, houses and brothers and sisters and mothers and children and lands (Mk 10:30). All I can say is that it has been a charmed life. No Cinderella story like mine! I have been conscious of the Lord's care, protection, and guidance every step of the way. I have seen God working in the marvelous convergence of circumstances, in the miraculous meshing of the gears. God has worked all things together for good.

So my testimony is that all His ways are pleasantness and all His paths are peace (Pr 3:17). My song is: "I bless the hand that guided, I bless the heart that planned." "It were a well-spent journey, Though seven deaths lay between."

The question often comes to me, "What could I want in life that I haven't had?" And the answer is always the same: "Nothing." My Lord has done all things well for me.

But there is a pain in my heart for those around me who are still living empty, wasted lives. I feel like the stricken deer in William Cowper's poem, saddened by the realization that most of mankind "find the total of their hopes and fears, dreams, empty dreams."

The Stricken Deer

I was a stricken deer that left the herd
Long since; with many an arrow deep infixed
My panting side was charged, when I withdrew
To seek a tranquil death in distant shades.
There was I found by one who had himself
Been hurt by the archers. In his side he bore,
And in his hands and feet, the cruel scars.
With gentle force soliciting the darts,
He drew them forth, and healed, and bade me live.

Since then, with few associates, in remote
And silent woods, I wander, far from those,
My former partners of the peopled scene;
With few associates, and not wishing more.
Here much I ruminate, as much I may,
With other views of men and manners now
Than once, and others of a life to come.
I see that all are wanderers, gone astray,
Each in his own delusions; they are lost
In chase of fancied happiness, still wooed
And never won. Dream after dream ensues;
And still they dream that they shall still succeed.
And still they are disappointed. Rings the world
With the vain stir. I sum up half mankind
And add two-thirds of the remaining half,
And find the total of their hopes and fears
Dreams, empty dreams.

NOTES

INTRODUCTION

1. L. S. Chafer, *Systematic Theology* (Dallas: Dallas Theol. Sem., 1947), p. 83.
2. See Gleason Archer, *A Survey of Old Testament Introduction* (Chicago: Moody, 1974), pp. 478-88.

CHAPTER 1

1. H. L. Mencken, quoted by Bill Bright, *Revolution Now* (San Bernardino: Campus Crusade, 1969), p. 15.
2. Will Houghton, "By Life or by Death." Copyright by Hope Publishing Co. Used by permission.
3. Author unknown, "Thou Alone, Lord Jesus," in *Hymns of Grace and Truth* (Neptune, N. J.: Loizeaux), no. 220.
4. Malcolm Muggeridge, *Jesus Rediscovered* (Garden City, N.Y.: Doubleday, 1969), p. 11.
5. W. J. Erdman, *Ecclesiastes* (Chicago: B.I.C.A., 1969), p. 11.
6. Robert Laurin, "Ecclesiastes," in *Wycliffe Bible Commentary*, ed. Charles F. Pfeiffer and Everett T. Harrison (Chicago: Moody, 1962), p. 587.

CHAPTER 2

1. B. E., "None but Christ Can Satisfy!" in *Hymns of Truth and Praise* (Fort Dodge, Iowa: Gospel Perpetuating Publ., 1971), no. 306.
2. From *The Children of the Night.*
3. Samuel Johnson, *The History of Rasselas, Prince of Abyssinia,* ed. J. P. Hardy (London: Oxford U., 1968).
4. Quoted by David R. Reuben, "Why Wives Cheat on Their Husbands," in *Reader's Digest* (Aug. 1973), p. 123.
5. Ralph Barton, quoted by Denis Alexander, *Beyond Science* (Philadelphia: Holman, 1972), p. 123. Used by permission of Lion Publishing.
6. E. Stanley Jones, *Growing Spiritually* (Nashville: Abingdon, 1953), p. 4.
7. *Choice Gleanings Calendar* (Grand Rapids: Gospel Folio Press).
8. Robert Jamieson, A. R. Fausset, and David Brown, *Critical and Experimental Commentary on the Old and New Testament* (Grand Rapids: Eerdmans, 1961), 3:518.
9. Jules Abels, *The Rockefeller Billions* (New York: Macmillan, 1965), p. 299.

CHAPTER 3

1. T. S. Eliot, "East Coker," in *Four Quartets* (New York: Harcourt Brace Jovanovich). Used by permission.

CHAPTER 4

1. James Russell Lowell, "The Present Crisis," in *Complete Poetical Works* (Boston: Houghton Mifflin, 1897), p. 67.
2. Cited by Henry G. Bosch, *Our Daily Bread* (Grand Rapids: Radio Bible Class, 24 May 1973).
3. Quoted by Bill Bright, *Revolution Now* (San Bernardino: Campus Crusade, 1969), p. 37.

CHAPTER 5

1. *Choice Gleanings Calendar* (Grand Rapids: Gospel Folio Press).

CHAPTER 6

1. H. C. Leupold, *Exposition of Ecclesiastes* (Grand Rapids: Baker, 1952), p. 141.

CHAPTER 7

1. G. C. Morgan, *Searchlights from the Word* (London: Oliphants, 1970), p. 217.

CHAPTER 9

1. Gilgamesh epic, quoted by H. C. Leupold, *Exposition of Ecclesiastes,* p. 216.
2. Denis Alexander, *Beyond Science,* pp. 132-33. Used by permission of Lion Publishing.

CHAPTER 12

1. Thomas H. Gill, "Lord in the Fullness of My Might," in *Hymns* (Chicago: Inter-Varsity, 1947), no. 26.
2. Fanny J. Crosby, "Saved by Grace," in *Hymns of Truth and Praise* (Fort Dodge, Iowa: Gospel Perpetuating Publ., 1971), no. 621.
3. Billy Barnes, "I Stayed Too Long at the Fair," (Hollywood: Tylerson Music, 1957). Copyright 1957, Tylerson Music Co. Used by permission.
4. E. Stanley Jones, *Is the Kingdom of God Realism?* (Nashville: Abingdon-Cokesbury, 1940).